Engaging Young Children in Museums

To the Founding Board of the Smithsonian Early Enrichment Center
for trusting me to bring their vision to fruition

Engaging Young Children in Museums

Sharon E. Shaffer

Left Coast Press Inc.

Walnut Creek, California

LEFT COAST PRESS, INC.
1630 North Main Street, #400
Walnut Creek, CA 94596
www.LCoastPress.com

ISBN 978-1-61132-198-2 hardback
ISBN 978-1-61132-199-9 paperback
ISBN 978-1-61132-200-2 institutional eBook
ISBN 978-1-62958-042-5 consumer eBook

Library of Congress Cataloging-in-Publication Data on file.

Printed in the United States of America

The paper used in this publication meets the minimum requirements of American National Standard for Information Sciences—Permanence of Paper for Printed Library Materials, ANSI/NISO Z39.48–1992.

Left Coast Press, Inc. is committed to preserving ancient forests and natural resources. We elected to print this title on 30% post consumer recycled paper, processed chlorine free. As a result, for this printing, we have saved:

2 Trees (40' tall and 6-8" diameter)
1 Million BTUs of Total Energy
177 Pounds of Greenhouse Gases
959 Gallons of Wastewater
64 Pounds of Solid Waste

Left Coast Press, Inc. made this paper choice because our printer, Thomson-Shore, Inc., is a member of Green Press Initiative, a nonprofit program dedicated to supporting authors, publishers, and suppliers in their efforts to reduce their use of fiber obtained from endangered forests.

For more information, visit www.greenpressinitiative.org

Environmental impact estimates were made using the Environmental Defense Paper Calculator. For more information visit: www.papercalculator.org.

Contents

Illustrations

Foreword

George Hein

The Smithsonian Institution, the world's largest museum complex (30 million visitors annually) has come a long way from its beginning over 150 years ago. The first Secretary, Joseph Henry, who directed the museum from 1846–1878, was dedicated to science and its progress and dissemination, but he did all he could to avoid having to take responsibility for a museum. The second Secretary, Spencer Fullerton Baird (1878–1887), devoted his career to making the Smithsonian a great national museum. It was under his administration that George Brown Goode, long recognized as a champion of museums as educational institutions, supported this goal, focusing on the value of museums for higher education. He wrote that museum visits were not likely to be educationally useful for young visitors in the "larval stage of development." The next secretary of the Smithsonian, Samuel Pierpont Langley (1887–1906), devoted enormous energy to creating a children's room in the Smithsonian's original building. He turned the south tower room of the castle into a colorful natural history exhibition with low exhibit cases so children could see the contents. He stipulated that labels should avoid Latin names, since these were of no interest to children. This groundbreaking gallery existed from 1901–1939. In subsequent decades, education increasingly devolved into separate activities in the growing number of museums within the Smithsonian Institution.

In the 1980s, under the leadership of the ninth Secretary Robert McCormick Adams, the Smithsonian launched two different educational efforts: the National Science Resource Center (jointly with the National Academy of Sciences) and the Smithsonian Early Enrichment Center. The former, now the Smithsonian Science Education Center, focused on elementary school science curriculum, creating major professional development programs for school districts nationwide and forming close alliances with industries interested in science education. The latter effort was a pioneering development in museum education for younger children. Originally serving 32 children in one location, it has grown to serve 150 children ranging from infants to kindergartners in three locations. Although its original population consisted primarily of children of Smithsonian employees, it always had a goal "to be a model lab school with a museum-based curriculum; a place that addressed the Smithsonian mandate for sharing knowledge."[1] Over its life it has increasingly emphasized and demonstrated the educational possibilities of museums for young children as described in this book.

Sharon Shaffer, founding Executive Director of the Smithsonian Early Enrichment Center, does not dwell on the complex origin of the SEEC that involved efforts by the Smithsonian's Women's Council and dedicated Smithsonian educators. Instead, she focuses on the theoretical background that underlies our increasing knowledge of how young children learn, what they learn, and how museums can best play an educational role in child development.

Developmental Theory is one of the great intellectual achievements of the past 150 years. That learning is more than pouring information into originally "empty vessels" but requires active interaction between individuals and their environment (including the social environment of learners with peers and teachers) is now well understood by researchers and recognized in principle by most educators. But our educational institutions, whether schools or designed informal settings (a broad field that includes museums), still have a long way to go to fully replace more traditional educational methods that linger on out of convenience, habit, or ignorance. To a large extent, museums that rely primarily on objects and interactive exhibits rather than texts and lectures have been freer than public schools to adopt progressive education methods and to embrace the constructivist educational ideals that Dr. Shaffer describes. Unfortunately, the training of museum educators—staff, docents and other volunteers—seldom sufficiently emphasizes what we know about how people, especially children, learn.

This volume traces the history of the advances in developmental psychology on education and its application to a particular population that has only in the past few decades been embraced in museums: preschool-aged children. Shaffer provides the theoretical background museum educators need in order to comfortably apply these educational methods and offers examples of museums that have adopted constructivist approaches for their educational programs.

The book's strength is in its detailed description of pedagogic methods for professional development for educators, with numerous examples of activities helping young children to become actively engaged with the objects they encounter in museums. It also implies the other component of progressive education: its socio-political aspect. Dewey emphasized that education in a democratic society had the dual role of helping children to develop intellectually through activity and to become conscious of their responsibilities towards society so that our society progresses towards more democracy. The other non-museum examples in the book—Maria Montessori's educational methods and the Reggio Emilia approach developed by Loris Malaguzzi along with working class parents in northern Italy—also had a goal of providing strong educational experiences for the poorer, underserved populations in their locations.

Sharon Shaffer's detailed explanation of advances in developmental psychology and its application to constructivist educational practices as well as her extensive experience in developing programming for preschool children make this book an important contribution to anyone wishing to engage this age group in museums.

Note

1. http://www.si.edu/seec/about (retrieved October 1, 2014)

Preface

*"If there's a book that you want to read, but it hasn't
been written yet, then you must write it."*

—Toni Morrison

For as long as I can remember I've had a passion for young children and learning. But my world changed dramatically on a single day in late June of 1988 when members of a task force at the Smithsonian Institution asked me to lead a new experiment in museum education as the founding director for what was to be the Smithsonian's model lab school.

Prior to that time my experience with young children was rooted in the realm of formal learning with an emphasis on early childhood education or, in today's vernacular, "early learning." By accepting the Smithsonian's offer I entered the museum world, stepping into a new way of thinking about education defined as informal learning. Within the intersection of these two spheres—early childhood education and museum learning—my understanding of young children's learning blossomed and developed over the next 25 years. My life was forever changed as I embarked on what was to be a remarkable journey, filled with excitement about the opportunity and a spirit of idealism.

The mandate to establish a national model in museum-based education for young children became the driving force that shaped my work and that of my colleagues within the Smithsonian Early Enrichment Center [SEEC]. The conversation articulating the mandate remains fresh in my mind, even with the passage of time. What I remember most was the acknowledgement by the committee that there would be little to guide us in achieving this directive since there were few, if any, programs in museums for this preschool audience. The task was daunting but at the same time exhilarating! What I discovered along the way was that there were, in fact, a few other museum-based preschools, each an experiment in early learning in museums.

This journey was one of constant learning, making sense of this new territory between the formal and the informal, the world of early childhood education and the world of museums. Along the way many books and articles informed my thinking and encouraged me to reflect on the museum experience. It was a journey marked by constant consideration of new ideas and growth through collaboration with peers in pursuit of the Smithsonian's vision of education for young children. We all gained so much from the experience, insight, and innovative practice of colleagues across the Smithsonian and the broader museum community.

Engaging Young Children in Museums represents a culmination of 25 years of experience in this place of intersection and consideration of the forces that shape education for our youngest museumgoers. It offers a broad perspective of early learning that includes history, theory, and practice.

There is great diversity within the field of museum education. For some educators this text will be a starting point as they begin the journey of early learning in museums; for others, it may validate practices. I hope the text prompts personal reflection for every reader with an eye toward reaching a higher level of quality in meeting children's needs in museums. While all the answers that educators seek will certainly not lie within the covers of this book, I hope that spending time with the ideas may serve as a catalyst for individual growth and the creation of new ways of thinking that lead to innovative practice.

My hope is that this book shines a light on the possibilities for serving preschoolers as well as their younger counterparts, and at the same time encourages museum practitioners to reach for the stars, open to the idea that the sky is the limit when it comes to connecting preschoolers and toddlers with the magic and wonder of museums.

Acknowledgments

It is with overwhelming gratitude that I acknowledge the generous support and contributions from early childhood experts, museum professionals, colleagues, and friends who encouraged and inspired this book. The passion for early learning that exists today is central to the message that this book shares.

I want to thank Dee Carlstrom Hoffman for sharing her enthusiasm and inspiration for young children and museums. I also want to acknowledge James Early for his support, insight, and belief in the value of early learning in museums.

In particular I would like to acknowledge Marjorie Schwarzer, Dan Driscoll, and Elee Wood for making a real difference through their work as editorial advisors. There are no words to express my appreciation for their expertise, support, and encouragement. Thank you also to Isabelle Alessandra, Heather Nielsen, Maria Marable, Lonnie Bunch, Heidi Hinish, and Donna Tobey for their thoughtful review of content.

Thank you to the voices from the field—Göran Björnberg, Kathy Danko-McGhee, Susan Day, Jo Graham, Kimberlee Kiehl, Pamela Krakowski, Ted Lind, Bonnie Pitman, Donna Tobey, and Jeanne Vergeront—for their generosity in sharing personal and professional insight on the future of early learning in museums.

A special thank you to the many museum professionals and early childhood educators for taking the time to share information about institutions, programs, history, and practice: Laura Huerta Migus, Laura Gottfried, Rachel Pucko, Ann Caspari, Anna Forgerson Hindley, Sarah Erdman, Melissa Covington, Megan Smith, Allison Wickens, Emily Blumenthal, Allison

Galland, Donna Mann, and Lotte Lent. A special thank you also goes to Mitch, Ryan, and Stephanie at Left Coast Press, Inc. for their commitment to excellence and support throughout the writing of this book.

Most of all I am grateful for the love and encouragement of my family: husband Mark, sons Stephen and Jason, daughter Andrea, and brother Scott, as well as to Chrystyna for her thoughtful feedback. It is with heartfelt thanks that I acknowledge my mother for her unconditional love and support throughout my life. My work is inspired by my grandchildren, who—like all young children—deserve the opportunity to experience museums fully. It is with deep appreciation that I dedicate this book to all the people important in my life.

SECTION ONE

Understanding the Audience of Young Children in Museums, Past and Present

Chapter One

Children and Museums: An Introduction

"Wonder is the beginning of wisdom."

—*Socrates*

Three- and four-year-olds sit in front of a painting at the National Gallery of Art, looking at a composition of line, shape, and color. They eagerly share their impressions of the artwork with their friends and with the educator from the museum. Although an art historian may see *The Bicycle Race* by Lyonel Feininger as a painting that requires visual interpretation because of its expressionist style, the children are readily able to construct their own meaning based on the shapes they see, easily recognizing bicycles and figures within the painting and understanding almost intuitively that this is a race. They enthusiastically contribute ideas to a lively discussion and ask questions that reflect a sense of wonder.

Figure 1.1. *The Bicycle Race* at the National Gallery of Art, Washington, DC. © 2014 Artists Rights Society (ARS), New York/VG Bild-Kunst, Bonn.

Introduction

[handwritten margin note: Museum's on children?]

In today's world it is not uncommon to see preschoolers in museum galleries. But a mere 20 years ago groups of preschoolers or families with young children rarely ventured inside art galleries or, for that matter, into most traditional museums. And though there were exceptions from pioneers in the museum field such as the Smithsonian Institution, young children rarely received attention and certainly did not hold a place of significance as an audience. In many cases these children were met with a less-than-pleasant greeting. In the past and even in some museums today, galleries other than those found in children's museums, or perhaps science centers, are more often thought of as a place for serious study or adult leisure rather than a place for young children.

Much has changed in the past 20 years. Many more museums are now welcoming preschoolers, yet there are still individuals with deeply held attitudes of the past that impede their museum's work with younger children, which I refer to as *early learning*. For many Americans, the term is not part of the average lexicon. According to the U.S. Department of Education, early learning references children from birth through kindergarten entry, although some organizations extend the range to children through age eight.

With a growing body of knowledge on early learning from research that examines neurological functioning in the first years of life to studies that explore the complex nature of cognitive development, museum professionals now have a new context for viewing young children and are more aware of the critical nature of the early years. Armed with this knowledge, they see early learning in a different light and thus are redefining *audience* to include younger visitors.

Engaging Young Children in Museums offers a framework for thinking about early learning in museums—science, history, and art museums; zoos and aquariums; children's museums; and more—and explores object-based methodologies that, based on my experience and the models I've observed in museums across the country and abroad, are effective in all disciplines as well as in early childhood classrooms. Although many educators are interested in the basic "how to" or practices that will contribute to the success of their programs, this text offers a broader foundation upon which to build early learning programs in formal and informal settings. It defines the current status of early learning in museums at a time when the topic is receiving national and international attention. But how did we as a nation and more broadly as a field get to this point, and where do we go from here? What do we really know about early learning in museums, and what defines best practice?

Early Learning: A National Conversation

Americans are engaged in a national conversation on early learning, a topic that is receiving widespread attention from politicians and policymakers to media experts and school administrators. From the influential to the everyday individual, people are recognizing early learning for its vital contribution to the nation, and support is growing, even from the highest levels of society. In 2013, a statement from the White House endorsed early learning as a high priority for the country:

> Expanding access to high quality early childhood education is among the smartest investments that we can make. Research has shown that the early years in a child's life—when the brain is forming—represent a critically important window of opportunity to develop a child's full potential and shape key academic, social, and cognitive skills that determine a child's success in school and in life. (White House 2014a)

President Barack Obama expressed his personal support for early learning by saying, "If we want America to lead in the 21st century, nothing is more important than giving everyone the best education possible—from the day they start preschool to the day they start their career" (White House 2014b).

This belief in the value of early learning, often referred to in the past as early childhood education, has been embraced by educators dedicated to teaching young learners and endorsed by the National Association for the Education of Young Children (NAEYC), an organization committed to high-quality education in the early years. NAEYC has a long history of advocacy and defines early childhood education as birth through age eight.

In the context of this book, the theories and practices described and illustrated primarily target children aged three to six years—preschoolers and kindergartners—but represent a broader spectrum of ideas applicable to younger and older children, often with specific examples. Museum practitioners working with young children need to be equipped with knowledge of learning theory and best practice to design programs or experiences appropriate for the audience. In fact, the idea of babies and toddlers in galleries requires knowledge of theory and appropriate strategies for engaging little ones, which draws on many of the same concepts discussed throughout this book.

Confluence of Events

Today's interest in early learning is a product of events of the past. This confluence of events—an increased focus on the field of early childhood education, brain research of the 1990s, and an emphasis on education and diversity in museums described in *Excellence and Equity* by the American Association of Museums (AAM 1992)—contributed to the rise of early learning. Just as educators glean insight from the history of museums more broadly, they are able to modify their thinking in light of new information from the more recent past.

Pivotal moments in time from the pioneering innovation of the Smithsonian Institution to the growth of children's museums as well as America's attention on social issues such as child labor, created a trajectory that informs practices in museums today, and establishes a foundation for the future. The museum field learned from the innovations and experimental designs of the past, from discovery rooms to sensory-based exploration, from the practices of children's museums and science centers, and discovered that the audience of young children is distinctly different in how meaning is constructed.

More and more, educators in the twenty-first century aptly perceive children not as naive and unsophisticated, a commonly held belief prior to and throughout much of the twentieth century, but as competent and capable learners with surprising cognitive abilities. But there are still many museum professionals not yet on board with this belief.

As museum professionals study educational theory and explore the early stages of cognitive development, they build a strong foundation for shaping practice in formal and informal settings. This is just as true today as in the past. And whether in classrooms or galleries, practitioners will be able to use knowledge about learning, which is critical for designing age-appropriate programs. Meeting the social, emotional, physical, and intellectual needs of children visiting museums or even exploring objects and art in other environments is a product of deeply understanding the characteristics of children as learners.

And while the focus may appear to be solely on the child, it is equally important to consider the child in a fuller context as a learner. Clearly, preschoolers do not arrive at the museum unaccompanied, but visit museums with adult companions, often with families—defined in many different ways—or with preschool groups. Educators familiar with theories of learning related to social interaction and scaffolding, such as Lev Vygotsky's view that learning is integrally linked to social interaction, will think about learning in the context of social relationships. For many in museums, this knowledge is often referred to in the context of family learning and the basis for supporting young children as they encounter art, artifacts, and scientific specimens or explore processes related to how the world works.

Research efforts in the 1980s and 1990s were expanding and reaching a broader public, which in turn informed thinking and practice around children. Major news magazines and papers featured stories on brain research and articles related to child development. Studies covered a wide range of topics with particular emphasis on linguistic and cultural diversity, early literacy, and play in addition to a wide array of themes related to development and learning.

NAEYC as an organization expanded its scope (Copple 2001) and shared findings from research with educators through its professional journal, *Young Children*. With a newly formed accreditation program created by NAEYC

(1985) and standards defining *developmentally appropriate practice,* early childhood educators could look to a set of principles to guide and engage children (Copple 2001). According to past NAEYC President Barbara Bowman (1980–1982), "Research has pointed with increasing clarity to the tie between how we care for and educate young children and their subsequent development and learning" (Copple 2001, p. 167). Research was a powerful force in shaping early childhood practice for the organization and was regularly featured in *Young Children.* The findings of experts from the field gave educators new ways of thinking about children and learning.

Studies in neuroscience documented what many educators had known intuitively through observation and experience: that the early years are significant in a child's growth and that interaction with the environment through multiple senses heightens learning. Many in education were attracted by research findings suggesting a link between the physiology of the brain and early sensory activity, including those in museums, and offered further reason to value and plan for early sensory interactions in museums.

Changes in the architecture of the human brain are the result of rich interactions with the environment, ultimately activating synapses that create neural pathways. Researchers learned that "those synapses that have been activated many times by virtue of repeated early experience tend to become permanent" (Shore 1997, p. x), an outcome many interpreted as an endorsement for early sensory experience.

Newly acquired information from research also indicated critical periods as nature's ideal time for development, but suggested that skills could be acquired at other times as well (Shore 1997). For example, researchers believe early exposure to sounds represented by spoken language and the ability to associate words with ideas is linked to a critical period and therefore should be encouraged for optimal development of a child's language skills. Knowledge of critical periods and the role of sensory experience in learning, along with findings related to the physical development of the brain, provides a rationale for increasing direct experience with sight, sound, taste, touch, and smell during early childhood as a means of increasing memory and strengthening future learning. Knowledge from brain research opened the door to new possibilities and perceptions about young children and learning.

It is important to remember that the idea of children in museums has changed significantly over time. Advocacy for young children in the twenty-first century refers primarily to children not yet in school, which is very different from the children visiting museums in the past. By the turn of the twentieth century, school-aged children, most often primary through secondary, gathered in museums for field trips, leading some professionals in the museum field to believe that children have always been served by museums. And while that may be true, younger children not yet in school were given little thought. Young children today—typically preschoolers, toddlers, and babies—have little in common developmentally with children entering museums throughout much of the twentieth century.

As scientists conducted research to gain insight into the function and neurological makeup of the brain, leaders from the museum field renewed their commitment to education by crafting a statement regarding the importance of serving more diverse audiences. *Excellence and Equity*, adopted by the American Association of Museums (renamed American Alliance of Museums in 2012) and written under the direction of Bonnie Pitman, Chair of the AAM Task Force on Museum Education, became a guide for museum practices and redefined education in the field after 1992. This discourse on diversity and focus on previously underserved (or in many cases nearly nonexistent) audiences in museums ultimately led to expanded programming for people of different cultures and varying ages and backgrounds, including a new interest in younger children. Framed by research and in light of the developing focus on diversity, a new vision of children arose within the museum community.

Interest from educators in museums grew, leading to innovative programs and exhibitions for young children. Experimentation in traditional museums brought early childhood concepts, such as play, to the public. The Strong Museum "targeted a broader audience with *One History Place* (1987), a hands-on recreated Victorian parlor for children seven and younger that gave them (and their parents) a feel for the era's overstuffed chairs, fussy tea sets, and fancy clothes, hand-laundering, scratch recipes, and do it yourself entertainment" (Eberle 2008, p. 267). Other museums experimented in similar fashion to address concepts relevant to younger audiences.

In the 1980s and 1990s, a new wave of museum-based programming for young children built on the work of early pioneers such as the Smithsonian Institution. Knowledge gained from research studies rekindled the spark and interest in developing programs for young learners, leading to new models in the field. The Smithsonian Institution established an early childhood program in 1988 with the intention of becoming a national model for museum-based education for young children. During the 1990s, the Smithsonian's lab school, the Smithsonian Early Enrichment Center (SEEC), gained recognition as a leader and advocate for early learning in museums. Educators at SEEC designed museum-based experiences for infants, toddlers, preschoolers, and kindergartners as part of the lab school experience and at the same time offered innovative seminars on a national level that explored teaching strategies focused on object-based methodologies.

By 2010 there were increasing numbers of museums serving preschoolers and also new efforts to create gallery experiences for infants and toddlers. This growing attention and commitment to a younger audience mirrored the prioritization of early learning within American society.

Changes since the last decade of the twentieth century fostered a new level of dialogue about education and diversity within the museum world. Individuals from a broad continuum of American society, including younger children, joined other visitors in exploring exhibitions and art galleries. It was a time for serious thought about early learning and the potential opportunities for engaging young museumgoers. It was also a time to reflect on social responsibility and the role of museums in the education of our nation's citizens, beginning with our youngest children.

Twenty-first Century Trends

The changing nature of museums was front and center as America entered the twenty-first century. The Partnership for 21st Century Skills, a "coalition bringing together the business community, education leaders, and policymakers . . . to kick-start a national conversation on the importance of 21st century skills for all students," created a framework defining an approach to teaching and learning to help students (K–12) master essential skills (P21 n.d.). Educators across formal and informal institutions, including museum professionals, incorporated this concept into their work.

At this time of change, museum professionals focused their attention on twenty-first century skills, redefined the role of the visitor in an attempt to balance the relationship between the museum object and the viewer, entered a dialogue on social responsibility, and brought research and evaluation into their midst with a priority that was lacking in the past.

With education at the forefront, museum organizations contemplated their role as educational institutions in a new century. A changing vision within traditional museums introduced a significant change to interpretation and the relationship between the visitor and the object. The original primacy of the object gave way to a shared role, with the visitor as a player in meaning making. This paradigm shift acknowledged visitors' prior knowledge and experiences as a contributing force in the interpretation and meaning making of objects. With this change came a blurring of roles between curators and educators as visitor engagement received greater attention.

This ideological shift toward greater inclusion and an emphasis on visitor ideas, needs, and experiences was a product of time and consideration. Czajkowski and Hill (2008) defined the museum as a model that was slowly "moving away from that of authoritative lecturer before a passive audience to that of a partner in dialogue with interested, engaged community members" (p. 255). Though slow in coming, this model was starting to inform the practice of many museums.

Dialogue within galleries was certainly an outcome of this new thinking about visitors and their role in the museum. As a result, social interactions became more a part of the museum experience in exhibitions and programming, supported by the earlier passion for Vygotsky's theory of social mediation.

Melinda Mayer writes in *From Periphery to Center: Art Museum Education in the 21st Century* (2007) about conversations in art museums as an approach that respects the visitor and the artwork and encourages informal conversation leading to exploration, questioning, storytelling, responsiveness, and meaning making in the gallery. She advocates building relationships of trust and mutual respect between museum educators and visitors to nurture learning and delight among art gallery visitors.

In the thought-world of education in the twenty-first century, the gap between informal and formal learning appears to be decreasing. At the same time, the conversation privileging early learning extends to all walks of life. Museums are increasing their efforts to serve younger children, which in turn shine a light on the issue of social responsibility.

Since the turn of the twenty-first century, the arts education field has demonstrated increased support for young children. In 2000, members of the National Art Education Association (NAEA) established a special interest group, Early Childhood Art Educators (ECAE), and drafted a position paper to define appropriate art practices for the early childhood years (ECAE 2000). ECAE leaders became strong advocates for young children, raising awareness through research and professional development.

Associations and professional journals highlighted early learning and made a case for greater community support for the nation's youngest citizens. The *Journal of Museum Education* recognized this important topic in its Spring 2012 issue, *Early Learning: A National Conversation*, with practitioners in the field sharing insights on research, policy, and programming.

Children's museums flourished nationally and internationally. They became important players and strong advocates for the education of young children within their communities, raising their profile from organizations complementing formal learning to ones of greater partnership with schools and neighborhood families. In a process of reimagining children's museums, the Association of Children's Museums (ACM) placed an emphasis on "sharing knowledge and capabilities with local resources and in supporting their constituencies—children" (ACM 2012).

Since the opening of the first children's museum a little more than a century ago, the concept of museums designed specifically for the young has become firmly entrenched in the marketplace, with nearly 400 children's museums currently serving communities worldwide, according to ACM Deputy Director Victoria Garvin. In 2012, ACM reported children's museums as "the youngest and fastest growing segment of the museum field as a whole" and confirmed data indicating 44% of its members opened in the 1990s and 82% opened since 1976 (ACM 2014a). This growth continues today and indicates interest and appeal for places designed specifically for children.

In 2003, ACM held the 21st Century Learner Symposium, a research-based forum that "brought the work of scholars, community partners, and national associations together to connect early learning to the creation of a lifelong learner" (Maher 2004). In 2013, the Institute of Museums and Library Services (IMLS) published a report, *Growing Young Minds*, linking early learning to museums and libraries. The report was a call to action for policymakers and practitioners to become more intentional in using the rich resources of museums and libraries "to give all children a strong start in learning" (IMLS 2013, p. 1).

Traditional museums are increasingly dedicating more time and resources to early learning, as evidenced by significant growth in the number of gallery programs for preschool and early elementary students. Aligning institutional programs with curriculum standards and offering professional development opportunities for classroom teachers has become commonplace for many cultural organizations. The conversation about STEM (science, technology, engineering, and mathematics) education, or the expansion of STEM to STEAM (which includes art), is now heard at museums of all types as well as schools. Much like children's museums, traditional museums are partnering with schools in new and different ways to bring content and learning strategies to students and teachers to enrich understanding.

In an effort to better understand learning in museums, the topic of research and evaluation surged to meet a renewed interest in documenting outcomes. It was no longer enough to track what was happening in museum galleries: the emphasis shifted to documenting the results of those experiences.

Discussions on research and evaluation led to the conclusion that museums needed to do more to understand practices in the field through research. Mary Ellen Munley's review of literature on early learning in museums clearly shows gaps in knowledge based on a lack of research (2012). In 2013, ACM added to the conversation and fostered an interest in research by bringing together experts in the field for the "Learning Value of Children's Museums Research Agenda Symposium" to define a field-wide research agenda for children's museums that identifies and synthesizes existing research about the learning value of children's museums (ACM 2013). Thinking about the role of the museum in shaping learning was at the forefront.

As boundaries between informal and formal learning continue to blur, leaders in the field will need to come together to define expectations and address key questions.

- What role should museums play in education that has traditionally been the responsibility of schools?
- What strengths do museums offer that are unique to these

institutions, yet relevant for children and teachers in more formal settings?

- In what ways can museums support and contribute to formal early learning?

These are questions yet unanswered, but that deserve time and attention.

There is dialogue within the museum field about social relevance and responsibility. In *Riches, Rivals, and Radicals,* Marjorie Schwarzer (2006) suggests "the American museum at last has discovered what it means to be a civic institution. Growing far beyond its early limitations, it has begun to understand its true potential to educate, inspire, and lead" (p. 27). A 2011 report, *Increasing Scientific Literacy: A Shared Responsibility* (Clough 2011), makes a case for museums and schools working together for the good of the community and the nation. The report suggests that the nation is at a critical juncture and acknowledges an overriding need for collaboration and coordination among agencies and institutions to build scientific literacy required for a strong America. At this time of great change, when museums are reimagining their role in society, our nation will be well served by further discussion on social responsibility as an integral part of the museum's mission.

As museums open their doors to this growing audience and take advantage of a national interest in early learning, our goal is to create experiences that are interesting, engaging, inspiring, and provocative.

Book Overview

Engaging Young Children in Museums is a blend of history, theory, and practice. It offers a framework for thinking about early learning in museums and the possibilities of what the future holds. There are three sections within this overview of children and museums:

- Section I: Understanding the Audience of Young Children in Museums, Past and Present
- Section II: Shaping Programs that Engage Children in Constructing Meaning
- Section III: Making a Difference: The Promise of the Future

The first section broadly examines the audience of young children, past and present, and focuses on how they make meaning in their world. This introductory chapter looks at today's reality of young children in museums and describes recent events that influenced the path that shaped the current context. The next section provides an overview of children in museums in the past century. My personal curiosity about the role of children in museums from the earliest days to current times led to chapter 2 ("The History of Children in Museums"). This look back in time tells the story of children in American museums, beginning with the marginalized status of very young children in the earliest museums of the mid-nineteenth century to field trips for a vast number of school students. It continues with a story of perseverance and dedication by individuals in the museum field, committed to creating special places and experiences for young museum visitors. The story of The Children's Room, housed in the Smithsonian's Castle, reflects the dedication of Samuel P. Langley, secretary of the Smithsonian Institution from 1887 to 1906. Langley's intent was "to excite the wonder and curiosity of children, to inspire them unconsciously with a love of nature" (Smithsonian Institution 1902) through personal connections with natural specimens and other objects. This is but one moment in history that has contributed to the changing landscape of museums. The shift in perception regarding the audience of preschoolers is almost unimaginable, and yet is documented by the history of the field.

Chapter 3, "Learning Theory and the Early Years," encourages us to think about learning theory as a foundation for practice. An examination of learning through four themes—experience, play, ways of knowing, and motivation—offers differing, yet often complementary views of the process of learning in the early years. Educational theories are relevant in a variety of contexts, crossing the boundaries between formal and informal learning. This knowledge presents a construct where professionals look beyond their own field to understand and learn from experts in related fields. For museum professionals, there is much to learn from the many years of research and practice in the field of early childhood education.

Section II moves the reader from theory to practice and builds on the idea that prominent early childhood models can inform museum practices. Chapter 4 examines models from Reggio Emilia to the Montessori Method and further explores practices such as the project approach, inquiry-based learning, arts-rich learning, and museum-based models, all representing ideas within respected programs of quality. The idea of best practice is examined in the remaining two chapters of this section, offering a framework for thinking about concepts essential to successful programming for young children, but at the same time acknowledging that best practice is dynamic and contextual. The preparation of educators and volunteers to act as effective leaders and facilitators for children's experiences in galleries and studios is explored in some depth.

The final section of the book looks forward and imagines possibilities for the future of young children in museums. It examines promising practices of today and considers the future of children in museums through the voices of leaders in the field, nationally and internationally, from formal and informal settings.

There have been many fine books that examine museum learning for children, and for that I am grateful. My goal in writing this book is to expand the scope and deepen the exploration of the topic by looking through the lenses of history, theory, and practice. The text offers a perspective that crosses boundaries between informal and formal learning, encouraging museum professionals to examine research and practice from the early childhood field as a source of knowledge to inform practice.

The future is bright for early learning. The spotlight is on the issue, and interest abounds across the nation. But what exactly does this mean for young children in museums? How will museums, with their dedication to informal learning, make a meaningful contribution to the education of our nation's children? How will the landscape of education in the United States need to change to leverage the rich resources available to make a difference in how children learn and possibly how teachers support learning? In the end, will our goal continue to be one that promises to engage, inspire, and create a sense of awe and wonder that leads to future learning, or will our goals shift with the ever-changing nature of our society? The answers to these questions and more are left to the reader, who hopefully will be inspired by the content of this book. For now, the journey begins with a closer look at the changing perception of children in society and in museums.

CHAPTER TWO

The History of Children and Museums in America: A Brief Overview

> "A child's world is fresh and new and beautiful, full of wonder and excitement."
>
> —*Rachel Carson*

The history of children in museums is a story that begins not with the opening of the first known museum in America in 1773, but more than a hundred years later on the National Mall in Washington, DC. The vision of Samuel P. Langley, Secretary of the Smithsonian Institution, brought an innovative idea to fruition with the opening of The Children's Room in the Smithsonian's castle in 1901 and created a space for children to experience the awe and wonder of the world through artifacts and natural specimens. This pioneering effort marked a milestone in the history of children in museums.

The Children's Room at the Smithsonian Institution

At the turn of the twentieth century, a museum dedicated to "the increase and diffusion of knowledge" sought to inspire, engage, and enlighten children through a space designed exclusively for young visitors. This visionary effort began in 1889—nearly 10 years before the opening of the Brooklyn Children's Museum (NeCastro 1988)—and resulted in the founding of The Children's Room in 1901 at the Smithsonian Institution, a traditional museum that emphasized scholarly research and exhibition of objects primarily for academic study. The perception of museums as a place reserved primarily for adults and older students was typical of its day. With the opening of The Children's Room, the Smithsonian was advancing an idea foreshadowing the future of museums, but far from the norm of the era.

Under the direction of Secretary Samuel P. Langley, who served from 1887 to 1906, the idea for The Children's Room was born. The idea for this dedicated area came after several disappointing attempts by Langley to shape exhibition spaces to better serve children. Langley's earlier effort was

Engaging Young Children in Museums, by Sharon E. Shaffer, 29–45. © 2015 Left Coast Press, Inc. All rights reserved.

Figure 2.1. The Smithsonian Children's Room. Smithsonian Institution Archives, image MAH–13391.

described as an "experiment in the ornithological department" (NeCastro 1988, p. 2), with exhibits of birds displayed for the children. Through this experiment, Langley recognized that "if children were to benefit from the educational possibilities which existed in museums, a different approach to exhibit design would be necessary" (NeCastro 1988, p. 2). To ensure the desired outcome, Langley named himself the honorary curator of the children's exhibit and prepared to oversee the work (NeCastro, 1988).

For Secretary Langley, the purpose of creating the children's space was "to excite the wonder and curiosity of children, to inspire them unconsciously with a love of nature" (Smithsonian Institution 1902, p. 54). The goal was inspiration, rather than instruction. Langley believed that creating a sense of wonder and nurturing curiosity would lead to learning.

The room itself was inspiring and reflected the philosophy of the day for planning effective environments for learning. Under the direction of DC architects Joseph Hornblower and James R. Marshall, structural changes were made to the space. Windows and doorways were modified to increase natural light and thereby create a more welcoming environment for children. A mosaic floor fashioned with brightly colored tiles added to the pleasant environment.

Interior designer Grace Lincoln Temple was responsible for the aesthetics of The Children's Room, carefully considering every aspect of the space. Contemporary theories of color, nature, and art were important in the decorative design and planning, reflecting principles of color harmony discussed in scientific journals of the time. She selected a color scheme of brilliant shades of greens and blues that covered the walls and ceiling. Stylized birds were stenciled into the ceiling design to continue the overall theme of nature. Even the detail of the ironwork was crafted with leaf-shaped forms (NeCastro 1988). The theme of nature within the space as well as the approach to color selection aligned with other educational theories prevalent during this time (NeCastro 1988).

With Langley's vision, and under the direction of Hornblower and Marshall, special exhibit cases were crafted so that younger visitors would be able to enjoy all of the objects on display. Latin words were removed from labels and simple text replaced scientific language.

Objects that had appeal for the young, primarily specimens from the natural world, became the heart and soul of The Children's Room. A rectangular aquarium sat in the center of the space surrounded by cases of birds, feathers, eggs, insects, minerals, and fossils at a child's height. Golden birdcages, four in all, hung from the ceiling and housed songbirds, canaries, and a hybrid goldfinch. The brilliant colors of the feathers and the music from the songbirds captured the attention of the children and added charm to the environment (NeCastro 1988).

Scientific illustrations of birds and other natural phenomena were displayed on top of exhibit cases. Visitors to The Children's Room also enjoyed the novelty of a large kaleidoscope designed by Langley. In keeping with the room's theme of nature, Langley constructed triangular tanks at the end of the kaleidoscope to hold live fish (NeCastro 1988). The immersive experience was rich in interesting objects to excite children and inspire questions about the natural world.

Langley's hope for young visitors was evident in the design and theme of The Children's Room. "Langley's guiding principle became his often repeated comment loosely paraphrased from Aristotle, that 'knowledge begins in wonder' a phrase which became the theme of the room and was painted on the transom above the south entrance" (NeCastro 1988, p. 5). Langley and the Smithsonian Institution's groundbreaking efforts recognized children as an important audience for museums and demonstrated a level of commitment that was unmatched in other traditional museums of its time.

But why did it take so long for children to be welcomed into the world of museums? The answer is complex but likely lies within social norms of America and the changing perception of childhood.

Changing Times

Throughout the nineteenth century and well into the twentieth century, American society perceived children primarily as naive and unsophisticated, and on the periphery. Children of the wealthy enjoyed a life of leisure and play, while for the most part children representing the lower socioeconomic strata of society were part of the work force at an early age with little time for formal schooling. But over the course of several decades, advocates for the young were challenging the idea of child labor and rethinking the rights of children. This story, captured in *Kids at Work: Lewis Hine and the Crusade Against Child Labor* (Freedman 1994), shows unimaginable treatment of children from poor families, many as young as three, and the burden they carried at an early age. Through Hine's startling photographs, the public could no longer ignore the circumstances allowed and encouraged almost universally across the nation.

> By the early 1900s, many Americans were calling child labor "child slavery" and were demanding an end to it. They argued that long hours of work deprived children of an education and robbed them of their chance for a better future. Instead of preparing youngsters for useful lives as productive adults, child labor promised a future of illiteracy, poverty, and continuing misery. (Freedman 1994, p. 2)

Through advocacy by individuals and groups fighting on behalf of children, expectations of the younger generation began to shift. It wasn't until "the Great Depression of the 1930s, a period of high unemployment" and "industry's growing needs for a better-educated work force" (Freedman 1994, p. 94) that the campaign against child labor accomplished real progress. The restrictions and limitations established through legislation were intended "to promote the rights and dignity of children and youth" (Freedman 1994, p. 97) and thus contributed to how children were viewed. No longer were children jettisoned into the adult world at an early age, leaving behind the few years of childhood and dependence.

Expectations for education were also changing. People began to challenge traditional views and develop progressive ideas about learning, which altered practices of the past and brought change to one of the most significant institutions within America: the school, a place revered for its ability to transform members of society and serve as a panacea for societal ills (Tyack and Cuban 1995).

The advent of progressive education ultimately influenced the attention paid to children and their place within society. These new ideas slowly gained authority in classrooms and in museums as seen in the development of The Children's Room at the Smithsonian, as well as the Brooklyn Children's Museum (1899) and the Boston Children's Museum (1915), "efforts that reflected progressive ideas concerning education" (NeCastro 1988, p. 1). Due to educational philosopher John Dewey and other advocates of sensory-based, experiential learning, the landscape of American society was shifting to reflect a new awareness of children and how they learn.

Social values of the time also influenced museums, along with other institutions of the early twentieth century, which led to a newly expanded relationship between museums and schools as part of a social progressive movement where serving the masses gained prominence. With industrialization and urbanization, and ultimately child labor laws and mandatory education, society's values reflected new perspectives. As museum field trips became the norm of the day for schoolchildren along with a newly emerging belief about youth and their role in society, museums were reimagined, providing museum experiences for more and more students across the nation.

Over time the image of childhood was no longer associated solely with the first six or seven years of life, but extended well beyond the teen years. The role of the child within the family took on new meaning and became embedded in a new way of thinking about children in society.

In looking back it is possible to see the impact stemming from social change contributing to the transformation of museums—past and present—and ultimately leading to a new relationship between children and museums.

The Early Days of the American Museum

Museums grew out of personal collections of the wealthy, where artifacts from travel abroad or personal interests were displayed in curio cabinets within the home and shared only with friends of a similar social class. Personal collections found their way to public spaces and at times were "often no more than a case of arrowheads or medical instruments . . . in the basements of libraries and colleges" (Schwarzer 2006, p. 8), but the artifacts were accessible to the public in a way that did not exist previously.

In 1773 the Charleston Library Society "gathered samples of animals, plants, and minerals from the South Carolina low country" (Schwarzer

2006, p. 8), establishing the first known American museum. Libraries were expanding their role in support of public education and a commitment to serving children.

Education was a common theme among museums and libraries with the goal of public enlightenment. This belief in education was evident in James Smithson's 1846 bequest to the United States for "the increase and diffusion of knowledge" for the purpose of creating a place dedicated to research and learning (Alexander 1996, p. 11), later to become the Smithsonian Institution. In many ways this commitment to education, echoed by most mission statements of early museums, shaped the identity of a new institution, the American museum.

As a public entity, the typical American museum of the late nineteenth century "was a collecting institution, organized in a hierarchical fashion" as "a place for the elite and privileged to teach the nation's working men and women what it meant to be cultured, civic-minded Americans" (Schwarzer 2006, p. 3). This desire to strengthen American democracy by building knowledge through instruction and entertainment, elevating the taste and moral condition of *the common man*, and serving as a catalyst for an artistic awakening became central to the mission of many museums (Zeller 1989). And although social progressives embraced the notion of *the common man* as representing the masses, many racial and ethnic minorities were still excluded.

Social attitudes and public response to those beliefs led to dynamic change within the American museum as an institution, a pattern that would be prominent throughout its history. The institution's deep devotion to education (Alexander 1996) would also take center stage and play out in galleries and schools across the nation.

As children began to visit museums in the early days as part of school journeys or field trips (Findlay and Perricone 2009), some in the museum field believed that the traditional exhibition design was less than perfect for children. This was the case for Secretary Langley at the Smithsonian Institution, but also for other pioneers in the field, and thus served as the impetus for designing a special place that recognized the unique learning style of the young and would afford greater opportunities for more personal exploration and discovery. This way of thinking led to the creation of the first children's museum in 1899 as well as other noteworthy efforts by more traditional museums to accommodate the younger visitor.

Children's Museums: A New Approach to Learning in Museums

Near the end of the nineteenth century a groundbreaking initiative building on Langley's work at the Smithsonian held great promise for catering to the interests and learning style of children: the development of children's museums. The realization that children were a unique audience with a distinct approach to learning led to a decision marking the beginning of what was to become an international movement. That decision would be credited to the Brooklyn Institute of Arts and Sciences and to the leadership of William H. Goodyear. Goodyear's innovative ideas came at a time of significant social change when concern over child labor was growing and increased support for public education was garnering favor. Within the next two decades mandatory school attendance became law in every state across America (Urban and Wagoner 2004), increasing awareness about the value of education.

As Curator of Fine Arts at the Brooklyn Institute, Goodyear traveled to Paris, where he was inspired by papier mâché models used for teaching biology. He believed that this visual approach was perfect for children in a museum setting. With the support of museum director William Hooper, the Brooklyn Children's Museum opened its doors in December of 1899 in the Bedford Park Building in Brooklyn. The initial collection came from a gift of less than perfect objects discarded by the Brooklyn Institute upon the move to its new building on Eastern Parkway. The objects from the Brooklyn Institute were deemed unsuitable for exhibition display (Din, 1998, p.15).

Objects in the early collection were selected to appeal to the interests of "young people between the ages of six and twenty years" (*Scientific American* 1900, p. 1) and to reflect the branches of knowledge taught in public schools at the time, reflecting in most cases the natural world. The collection was intended to give life to classroom concepts and to offer opportunities for discovery through visual experiences and exhibitions related to nature. To bolster the collection, a set of Emile Deyrolle's models—primarily art drawings of flowers, plants, and insects—were purchased from a Paris publishing company to ensure that students experienced educational materials of high quality and guaranteed that the museum had more than discarded objects (Din 1998, p. 16).

Goodyear's advocacy led to future acquisitions of natural specimens useful for the instruction of children. While the procurement of natural objects supported the study of botany, zoology, geology, meteorology, and human anatomy, other artifacts were acquired for instruction in geography and history (Din 1998).

The early popularity of the Brooklyn Children's Museum was rooted in the freedom given to individual students to follow personal interests and pursue knowledge based on instinct. Nurturing innate curiosity was considered essential to the museum experience. Teachers and students also enjoyed the museum's simple gallery activities such as staff reading to small groups of schoolchildren, illuminating the mysteries of the world. Teachers favored the museum's visual materials and believed that the approach enhanced the learning of complex concepts.

The hands-on discovery approach typically associated with children's museums was not a part of the original concept, but was introduced by Anna Billings Gallup following her 1902 appointment to the Brooklyn Children's Museum as a curatorial assistant. Under Gallup's direction, a set of "minerals to sort, polish, and examine" (Hein 2006, p. 166) offered young visitors tactile experiences while staff lectures on natural and social sciences supported student learning through the other senses. Gallup recognized that children were active learners and believed strongly in following the child's major interests.

> [We] must remember that the keynote of childhood and youth is action. Any museum ignoring this principle of activity in children must fail to attract them. The Children's Museum does not attempt to make electricians of its boys, nor is its purpose to do the work of any school. The object is rather to understand the tastes and interest of is [sic] little people and to offer such help and opportunities as the schools and homes can not give. (Gallup 1908 in Hein 2006, p. 167)

Through this active process of exploration and discovery, the museum experience was intended to encourage "their [the children's] powers of observation and reflection" (Hein 2006, p. 166) and to bring them into contact with artifacts relevant to their everyday lives.

The opening of the Brooklyn Children's Museum was a landmark innovation that led to other community museums, including the innovative

Figure 2.2. Kids and turtle at the Brooklyn Children's Museum, 1931. Courtesy of the Brooklyn Children's Museum Archive, all rights reserved.

Boston Children's Museum. As with its predecessor, the Boston Children's Museum drew upon the natural world for gallery displays and established new practices that would become integral to the future of museums.

Under the direction of the museum's president, Dr. Charles Douglas, the experience of visiting a museum shifted from the passive stroll through galleries to a more active role of children as learners. He believed that children experienced a newfound joy of observation and discovery through innovative interpretative techniques designed to enhance understanding of natural phenomena (Douglas 1921). His attention to visual education led by a cadre of trained docents was the product of a belief that facilitated learning resulted in greater meaning and that "phenomena are made understandable" through this guided experience (Douglas 1921, p. 161).

As an advocate for children and museums, Douglas encouraged all museums to develop departments specifically to serve children. He also believed that every museum should invest in and value docent services. Although groundbreaking for the time, Douglas's ideas would be widely accepted by many professionals in the museum community by the end of the twentieth century.

The groundbreaking efforts of the Brooklyn Children's Museum along with the pioneering ideas introduced by the Boston Children's Museum established a legacy that identified these institutions as special places for young learners. The mission associated with today's children's museums continues to reflect the original belief that space should be designed to reflect developmental needs of the young. The idea that "children learn through play and exploration, in environments and experiences designed just for them" (ACM 2014b) fits well with the beliefs of the early pioneers encouraging exploration and discovery based on children's interests.

Museums and Society

In the formative years of museums few were more committed to populism than John Cotton Dana. The innovative founder and director of the Newark Museum in 1909, Dana showed support for the community, particularly minorities, which led to special exhibitions relevant to these groups. Dana also recognized children as an important audience and encouraged museums to set aside space dedicated to "a group of objects and pictures selected, installed, and labeled with special references to the interests of young people" to arouse curiosity and attract children to collections (Peniston 1999, p. 163).

The Toledo Museum of Art demonstrated a similar interest in children and in 1914 created a teaching exhibition as part of a City Beautiful Campaign intended to bring art to all classes and ages. Flower and vegetable seeds were sold to accompany a lecture on gardening for children. The museum further touched the lives of the young through a Bird Campaign for schoolchildren, engaging young visitors through lectures, workshops for making community birdhouses, and exhibitions documenting the habits and migration of birds (Zeller 1989).

While the belief in civic responsibility was common during the early twentieth century, not all leaders in the field embraced the social agenda of museums that included public education. Benjamin Ives Gilman of Boston's Museum of Fine Arts expressed his beliefs about the aesthetic mission of museums in *Museum Ideals of Purpose and Method* (1918). Gilman, known for saying "a museum of art is primarily an institution of culture and only secondarily a seat of learning"(Zeller 1989, p. 29), recognized that the artifacts and natural specimens in other museums might be more adaptable for instruction. It might seem at first that Gilman was indifferent to education in the museum, but in fact he contributed significantly to the field and is recognized today for those contributions (Zeller 1989). His introduction of museum guides in 1907, which he called *docents* (Alexander 1996), would have a long-lasting impact on education in museums.

During this era a general commitment to education was apparent as museums served schoolchildren through free public lectures, loaning teaching objects and collections to schools, special tours, and exhibition spaces crafted for the school-aged visitor. The intention was to enlighten and captivate the curiosity of schoolchildren through museum experiences primarily with artifacts and scientific specimens. Libraries were similarly interested in education as evidenced by the work of librarian Henry Watson Kent, one of the first to invite schoolchildren to visit a public exhibition at the library, thus establishing a tradition of school tours and programming by museums (Schwarzer 2006).

In step with this dedication to learning, the Metropolitan Museum of Art introduced "Story Hours for Children" in which young visitors 4 to 15 years of age listened intently to stories that "correlated with the treasures in different parts of the museums" (*New York Times* 1918):

> There is a strange sight every Sunday afternoon a little before 3 o'clock on the upper part of Fifth Avenue—hundreds of children, all of them smiling, flocking through the great doors of the Metropolitan Museum of Art. "The Pied Piper must have just passed along," the grownups say, but it is really something more wonderful than that, for the children are going to the museum of their own accord, to study art. (*New York Times* 1918)

The social movement influencing museums during the early twentieth century was also apparent in public schooling. Old-school, educational practices were being challenged by John Dewey, an educational philosopher in America best known for his ideas of learning by doing. He criticized the passive approach of memorization and recitation in schools and the lack of relevance to everyday life. He emphasized the need to align education with the democratic process and defined this critical link between school and society in his writings (Dworkin 1959). Dewey also brought recognition to the value of museums and integrated museum experiences into the Lab School at the University of Chicago. For his students, the galleries of Chicago's museums were a place of learning every day.

At this same time, Maria Montessori's ideas of education were growing in acceptance. She believed that learning occurred through sensory experiences, teachers should be facilitators rather than lecturers, and independence should be encouraged. It was her focus on child-centered learning and her ultimate respect for the child that resonated with children's museums and influenced education inside and outside of classrooms. John Dewey and Maria Montessori held many similar beliefs and contributed to the progressive education movement that touched museums and schools.

The early days of the museum shaped the future of the institution. Pioneers in the field envisioned museums as places that would serve communities and almost without exception, acknowledged education for its essential role in society.

Museums and School Partnerships

In the late nineteenth and early twentieth centuries, museums opened their doors to school-aged children and developed school partnerships to bring artifacts, slide shows, and experts to classrooms (Findlay and Perricone 2009). This commitment to education was realized not only through programs within the walls of museums, but also in classrooms in the public school sector. Through these partnerships, museum practice and ideology reached a broad spectrum of students.

As early pioneers, the Buffalo Society of Natural Sciences (New York), the Davenport Academy of Natural Sciences (Iowa), and the American Museum of Natural History (New York) demonstrated their interest in supporting public education through school field trips, described as *school journeys*, and loan programs (Findlay and Perricone 2009). Curators created special tours and lectures that offered students tactile experiences with natural specimens and opportunities to study artifacts on display in the museums. Lectures, slide shows, and object lessons encouraged an active approach to learning easily supported by museum collections.

Partnerships between museums and schools broadened student horizons through exposure to unique artifacts of the day. William Powell Wilson, founder of the Philadelphia Commercial Museum, and Edward Brooks, superintendent of Philadelphia schools, changed the study of geography and culture for students (Findlay and Perricone 2009) through museum collections. This exemplary partnership "turned the museum into a source of inspiration and information for teachers and students" (Findlay and

Perricone 2009, p. 9) and through an experimental program "supplied artifacts, specimens, and expertise to schools and state teachers colleges" (Findlay and Perricone 2009, p. 10).

The Great Depression brought new opportunities to unite museums and schools with the Works Progress Administration (WPA) Museum Extension Project (1935–1943). " By 1934, the nation's school spending had declined by 34 percent from pre-Depression levels" (Findlay and Perricone 2009, p. 49). Cuts in school resources were replaced by museums and support from WPA programs. Visual aids crafted by the many unemployed artisans and craftsmen represented many diverse formats and were designed to enrich curriculum. For example, "posters, dioramas, puppets and marionettes, architectural models" (Findlay and Perricone 2009, p. 39) as well as other visual aids were created through the Pennsylvania Museum Extension Project (PMEP), reaching more than a million and a half visual aid materials at the peak of production (Findlay and Perricone 2009, p. 39). The Museum Extension Project increased access to visual aids in schools, developed school journeys, supported museums in their everyday work, provided docents or interpreters to museums, and established children's museums in schools.

Figure 2.3. Set of Peter Rabbit puppets, Works Progress Administration, Pennsylvania Museum Extension Project, ca. 1935–1943. Courtesy of Broward County Library, Bienes Museum of the Modern Book, Fort Lauderdale, Florida.

Museums would continue to invest in education and value partnerships with schools. But as society's views of childhood changed, museums would eventually go outside the boundaries of formal schooling (K–12), but not for some time. By the turn of the twenty-first century, museums would seriously consider preschoolers and kindergartners as a target audience; a mere decade later, they would consider toddlers and babies as a possible audience for the museum.

A Changing World: A New Perspective for Museums

In the years following the end of World War II and in an era of declining patronage, museums gained in popularity and visits increased dramatically, including a rise in field trips through public schools with the onset of the first group of baby boomers (Schwarzer 2006). This was also a time when mainstream educational institutions returned to more traditional teaching practices, leaving the ideas of John Dewey and his progressive colleagues behind. Museums responded in similar fashion, which led cultural institutions to favor a more didactic approach rather than the hands-on practices of the first half of the twentieth century.

In the years following the 1957 launch of Sputnik by the Russians, the country looked to educational reform as a panacea for addressing its political failings on the world stage (Tyack and Cuban 1995). Americans struggled with the idea that a competing nation might indeed become a world power greater than the United States. To regain its role as the clear leader of the world, America entered the race to space with a sense of urgency (Schwarzer 2006) and reinvigorated its commitment to science education. Education, with particular emphasis on science and mathematics, gained primacy in almost every facet of society, forging the development of science museums to encourage and strengthen knowledge of scientific thinking and principles. New institutions from planetariums to science centers joined in teaching America's youth about mathematics and physics through programs and exhibitions, thereby supporting this national effort.

A notable contribution to science education in museums came from Frank Oppenheimer, a physics professor who gained acclaim for his innovative approach to museum exhibitions. His conceptual framework relied on a more interactive experience of exploration and discovery for museum visitors intended to bridge the knowledge gap in science and technology between the layperson and the expert (Oppenheimer 1968). In many ways, exhibitions developed around Oppenheimer's ideas at the Exploratorium in San Francisco were designed to mirror laboratories where museum visitors would be able to explore and observe, taking an active role in their own learning to gain deeper understanding of scientific principles. And while this approach to science was intended for a broad range of visitors, the underlying principles would ultimately have particular significance for children visiting museums.

Discovery Rooms: Special Spaces for Interactive Experience

Frank Oppenheimer's declaration that sensory perception is essential to learning influenced museum practices across the field, building a foundation for the concept of hands-on discovery rooms. Museum educators across the country witnessed a growing interest in this model and recognized the value of learning through exploratory, sensory experience. With the introduction of discovery spaces, museums were offering learning opportunities that catered to the learning style of children.

The 1960s work of Michael Spock, then director of the Boston's Children's Museum, offered yet another model for traditional museums to ponder. His groundbreaking approach emphasizing "experiential learning and the joys of touching" (Madden and Paisley-Jones 1987, p. 2) mirrored earlier ideas of progressive education and again brought greater prominence to the concept of tactile experiences for museum visitors. His work encouraged museum practitioners to think about possibilities for incorporating similar experiences into the traditional museum setting.

In fact, experiential learning was crossing boundaries in Fort Worth, Texas, where in 1968 the state's first children's museum was redefining itself as the Fort Worth Museum of Science and History, blending practices from children's museums with galleries reminiscent of more traditional museums. This newly imagined museum welcomed audiences of all ages but retained the highly attractive practice of offering hands-on experiences with artifacts as a natural part of the museum visit (Smith 2011). The time-honored practices of children's museums were penetrating the world of more traditional museums.

Many traditional museums translated the ideas of Oppenheimer and Spock into discovery spaces designed exclusively for more personal interaction with artifacts and scientific specimens. While this hands-on approach was considered an important methodology for serving children, it was equally popular with all ages and dramatically changed the nature of personal exploration in museums for all visitors.

In the late 1960s, The Touch and See Room at the James Ford Bell Museum "was looking for a way to make the museum more accessible to young children" (Murdock 1987, p. 14) and thus developed a space encouraging visitors to explore and learn from natural history specimens. Similar to The Children's Room at the Smithsonian Institution, labels were discarded in favor of individual meaning making through a process of observation and questioning. A new feature of The Touch and See Room was certainly an open invitation to touch specimens from the collection selected intentionally for this environment. Horns and antlers, an elephant skull, and animal skins were objects that delighted children in visits to the discovery space. The founders of The Touch and See Room were hopeful that visitors would develop an interest in nature through their personal experiences in the discovery room and then pursue those interests in the museum and in their lives (Murdock 1987).

The Discovery Room at the Smithsonian's National Museum of Natural History followed soon after in 1974, becoming a model for a touch exhibit within a traditional museum setting (Marsh 1987). During this time museums across the nation explored the *discovery idea* and experimented with various options for integrating the touch experience into the museum environment.

As innovative leaders developed the concept of discovery space, many museum professionals shared the excitement and lent support. This interest, however, was not universally embraced. Museum professionals representing various roles within institutions were concerned that certain cultural norms associated with museum experiences—in particular, looking rather than touching—might break down when visitors were invited to touch objects during the museum experience. Even as these concerns were raised, the appeal of this novel approach within the museum setting gained traction.

Prior to the approval of its discovery space, the Smithsonian's National Museum of Natural History had similar concerns within the ranks of the museum, but by 1972 the project moved forward with funding from the National Science Foundation (NSF) and opened two years later. A shared belief in this innovative concept as "a new kind of learning experience in museums" was the tie binding the two organizations: the museum and the funder (Marsh 1987, p. 4). The public's interest in touching authentic objects was cited as one of the most important reasons for the success of this newly emerging museum model.

With the support of the National Endowment of the Arts, the Florida State Museum pursued an innovative approach similar to the discovery space offered by the Bell Museum. The Object Gallery, designed for self-directed study, opened in 1974 with a variety of artifacts accessible to the public, some on view in the more traditional fashion and others that allowed for personal touching (Whetzel 1987). Live animals were included in the gallery to arouse curiosity and connect to research in animal behavior. A constant flow of artifacts led to a changing environment and a personal experience that reflected exhibitions in the museum itself, an approach intended to draw visitors into the space over and over again (Whetzel 1987).

The availability of federal funding dramatically changed education in the early 1970s. Reflecting social values of the time, funds were tied to programs serving disadvantaged youth (Blackmon 1987) and more diverse audiences. Social responsibility gained primacy and museums joined others in responding to social issues, returning to a practice that was more highly favored in the first part of the century.

The Field Museum of Natural History (Chicago) mirrored the practice of other museums by expanding its programming to serve more diverse audiences and designed an exhibit on the senses where visitors were invited to explore objects through sight, sound, touch, and smell (Blackmon 1987). The Place for Wonder finally opened in 1977 and offered a sensory-rich exhibit experience that encouraged direct contact with objects in the collection, a new way of thinking about visitor experiences in museums. Additional programs with interpreters in the galleries grew from lessons learned during this experimentation with visitor learning. The learning needs of children were certainly met through this initiative.

Natural history and science museums were not the only museums interested in the discovery idea. The Smithsonian's National Museum of American History joined the ranks of museums experimenting with the discovery approach and applied the concepts to learning history in a space that would become known as Hands-On History. The central theme of this interactive space highlighted methodologies used by historians to gain knowledge about the past and then encouraged visitors to become the historian by using artifacts or reproductions to construct meaning about a different time and place. Space and activities were carefully designed to encourage a blend of hands-on activity and social dialogue intended to shape the visitor's experience. Actual artifacts and carefully crafted reproductions—from a sugar cone to a small bucket called a *piggin*—focused attention on concepts related to eighteenth-century America and allowed visitors of all ages to explore the past in a meaningful way. Although the activities targeted children aged nine and older, there were several age-appropriate experiences for younger siblings. *From Sheep to Mittens* encouraged younger children to "trace the steps in wool processing, from shearing the sheep to knitting the final product" (Sharpe 1987, p. 9). Visitors of all ages were able to examine a small collection of artifacts from Colton's Store to identify the use of each object from the past and consider its counterpart today.

By 1985 an inventory revealed "more than one hundred museum spaces which used the discovery idea," (Madden and Paisley-Jones, 1987, p. 2). Museums were showing a growing interest in more interactive experiences and offering meaningful ways to engage children in learning as a result.

A common theme across discovery spaces, regardless of their place or name, was the critical role of the docent in supporting visitors and facilitating their experience, an idea modeled on practices from the Boston Children's Museum in the early part of the twentieth century. In today's terms, the approach was one of *scaffolding*, which intended to increase learning and allow for higher levels of success through the support of a more knowledgeable partner in learning. The goal of exploration was always to go beyond the simplicity of naming or labeling an artifact or a natural specimen for the purpose of developing a more complex understanding of the object. Thoughtful questions posed by docents were intended to expand the thought process and engage in conversation to heighten the visitor's experience.

Oppenheimer's belief in learning through the senses became a reality in many museums. His innovative approach led directly to the formation of discovery spaces in science centers like the Omniplex Science Museum (Oklahoma City), but ultimately became an accepted approach to more exploratory learning that can be found today in museums with collections representing almost every discipline. A more personal connection to learning and a greater understanding of concepts is the perceived benefit for visitors, a goal aligned with museums' educational missions.

Conclusion

The history of museums offers insight into the primacy of education within the institution. From the early days museums demonstrated their commitment to schoolchildren, laying the groundwork for welcoming younger visitors to the museum in the future. With innovations such as the children's museum and initiatives by more traditional museums to design spaces and experiences that would capture the hearts and minds of younger visitors, the museum as an institution charted a new path.

At each step along the way, new opportunities emerged to enliven museums, doing so in a way that emphasized a learning style natural for children and supporting a sense of wonder and discovery. Museum–school partnerships, discovery rooms, tactile gallery experiences, and special programs ultimately changed the landscape of museums, setting the stage for future innovation.

The museum community is ever-changing, as proven by the many emerging programs for this audience of young learners; yet, there is still much to learn. Are our practices effective? Do they represent a quality experience that contributes in a positive way to the child? What outcomes are we anticipating and how are we evaluating our efforts?

Change continues today with developing views about learning, perceptions of children, and beliefs about the role of the institution within society. As we look to the future, we can be certain that change will continue to be on the horizon.

CHAPTER THREE

Learning Theory and the Early Years

> "Education is the kindling of a flame, not the filling of a vessel."
>
> —*Socrates*

Introduction

As museum professionals enter the realm of early learning, whether it be in designing exhibitions and gallery spaces or creating educational programs, having background knowledge in learning theory contributes to the experience that the museum will offer. Understanding experience, play, ways of knowing, and motivation in relationship to learning grounds practice and influences how we value and therefore advocate for different approaches to experiences in museums.

So often educators and others that touch the lives of young children work from a point of intuition, which is a wonderful place of reference, but is not sufficient for the important work to make a difference in children's learning. As professionals it is vital to read, reflect, interpret, and think critically about educational theory to better understand the audience of young children to create engaging and meaningful experiences. Early learners deserve a place in museums with opportunities to explore, imagine, and create memories that engage the body, mind, and spirit.

Museum professionals need to think about the role of theory in practice and contemplate why it matters. Why is theory important in education? What theories or beliefs contribute to our understanding of learning in museums, particularly related to young children, and who are the experts articulating theories that deserve attention? Devoting time to these questions will ground practice and strengthen understanding of early learning in museums.

Learning Theory in History

From the ancient Greeks to the present, theories about learning play a role in society and define education in all of its complexity. Some ideas have withstood the test of time and continue to be valued in schools and other institutions today, whereas others were popular in their day, but faded with the introduction of new ideas.

Names of certain theorists can be found within our everyday vernacular—Dewey, Piaget, Montessori, Gardner—while others are less well known. And yet the ideas proposed by unrelated and diverse thinkers across time—the familiar and the less known—seem to fall into clusters, each group representing ideas or themes that intertwine and build on one another. Making sense of the vast array of theories can be confusing to an educator new to the field and at times can challenge the experienced educator to examine ideas more closely. Within any institution it is important to know and understand the set of beliefs that guide learning and practice.

Ideas that emerge from the research in the past century serve as a foundation for today's thinking about best practice in museums. As each topic related to learning theory is examined, consider the connection to designing current programs and exhibitions.

- How will theories lead museum professionals and gallery facilitators to plan appropriate and engaging experiences for children in museums?
- What underlying principles will guide professionals in designing museum environments?
- Which theories are essential building blocks for developing early learning programs that are age appropriate and nurture a young child's curiosity?

For the museum professional new to educational theory, this overview is important to explain the *why*, the rationale that informs practice. Knowing what to do is only half of the equation; knowing why is equally important. Theory is essential to the conversation about early learning and a starting point for educators as they plan for children.

In this chapter I examine critical topics related to learning theory through the lens of certain themes—experience, play, ways of knowing, and motivation—and focus on what the experts say about learning. For some educators this will serve as a refresher, while for others it is an introduction to the ideas and beliefs that are respected within the field. Theory does not exist in a vacuum, but is embedded in the real world. To make those connections clear, ideas from theory are referenced throughout the text, often with examples to illuminate and clarify practice. The hope is that readers will be inspired to learn more about educational theory and extend their quest for knowledge beyond the covers of this book.

Educational Theory

Research and theory inherently suggest specific strategies for supporting young children in learning. Techniques are a natural outcome of theory if they reflect behaviors and patterns of learning visible in the lives of young children. For example, children are active learners, constantly exploring and engaging with their environment. Techniques that actively engage children, such as touching objects, role play, puzzles, block building, and sharing ideas, are a reflection of the natural inclination and behaviors of this audience. The goal is to align practice with theory and to appreciate the characteristics of young children.

George Hein provides one of the most respected models for understanding theory as a concept in *Learning in the Museum* (1998). Hein outlines four domains, each representing a different category of educational theory, and defines values and beliefs about knowledge ascribed to each domain. This model is an excellent starting point for educators to reflect on theories of learning and how they intersect with beliefs about knowledge. Ultimately, this model is important because it offers a useful overview of theory for practitioners.

According to Hein, "an educational theory requires a theory of knowledge (an epistemology); it requires a theory of learning; and finally, a theory of teaching, the application of the conceptions about how people learn and what it is they learn" (1998, p. 16). By breaking educational theory into three components, Hein allows educators to grapple with one element at a time before looking toward the intersection of ideas. In defining each quadrant by specific teaching strategies— didactic, stimulus-response, discovery, and constructivism—he further adds elements that define each theoretical perspective, some of which are familiar.

Each category or theory is defined by a set of beliefs and values, all of which align with one another to preserve continuity, which occurs when ideas support one another rather than conflict. For example, a theory that identifies independence as an aim for learners and at the same time prescribes every precise action in the process of learning creates disequilibrium or internal conflict. Clearly the ideas do not align. Ideally, beliefs and values within a theory should support one another, not create tension.

As described by Hein (1998), beliefs about the nature of knowledge exist along a continuum from *realism*, the belief that knowledge exists in the real world without connection to interpretation, to *idealism*, where knowledge is uniquely constructed within the individual. This concept, while challenging for a novice to comprehend, has value in determining what approach to teaching and learning makes sense for the organization. A didactic approach to teaching, such as a lecture, works if one believes that knowledge is constant in the world, but may or may not fit with a belief that knowledge is uniquely created within each individual. Similar to knowledge, beliefs about learning also fall along a continuum, from learning defined as passive and incremental to learning viewed as "active, leading to restructuring of the mind" (Hein and Alexander 1998, p. 33).

To better understand theories of learning, it is possible to place teaching methodologies in quadrants formed by the intersection of beliefs about

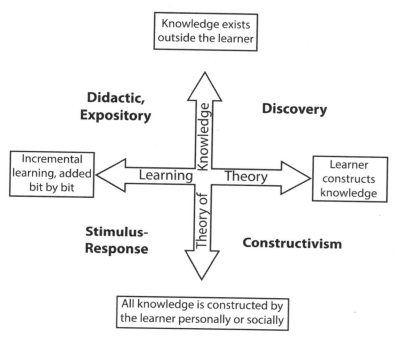

Figure 3.1. Hein's model for educational theories. Redrawn from Hein 1998.

knowledge and learning. Hein (1998) offers an excellent model for understanding how these theories intersect. It is probably this aspect of the model that creates the most interest for educators. So often there is a desire to know *what to do* and less thought to *why*. By investing time in Hein's model, it is possible to find answers to both questions based upon personal beliefs about learning.

Hein's model introduces theories of knowledge on a vertical axis that intersects with theories of learning on a horizontal axis. Quadrants describe different approaches to teaching. A common teaching approach known as discovery is located in the top right quadrant. A discovery approach to knowledge is perceived as existing outside of the learner (*realism*), and the process of learning is active. Discovery learning values active participation through personal, hands-on exploration and results in a specified outcome.

Discovery is familiar to many museumgoers, particularly those visiting science centers and children's museums, but is also apparent in hands-on history rooms and discovery carts designed for firsthand exploration of artifacts. An activity that encourages critical thinking as a means to match artifacts of the past with similar objects representing today's culture is an exercise of discovery. Children engage in problem-solving as they decode clues to draw conclusions about the purpose of each object with an end goal for finding objects that match. The process is about individual discovery, but the outcome is defined in a specific way.

Discovery is clearly an approach that should receive attention from anyone interested in early learning. The natural inclination of young children to explore their world as a way of knowing fits with the concept of learning as an active process.

Another more traditional and familiar method of teaching—lecture—falls into the didactic, expository quadrant. This method recognizes knowledge as a constant in the real world, but sees learning as something acquired in an incremental fashion from a more knowledgeable external source. Traditional teaching is construed as a didactic or expository approach in which the teacher imparts her knowledge through lecture. This is probably the most well-known method of teaching, one that many adults experienced as students. At the same time, this approach is the least accessible for early learners who are naturally active and constantly on the move.

Returning to the opening quote for this chapter, a didactic approach such as lecture represents the *filling of a vessel*, whereas discovery is more closely aligned with the *kindling of a flame*. Discovery is active, whereas didactic methods are more passive for the learner, but in both cases there is intent to acquire specific knowledge that exists in the real world.

Teaching strategies at the opposite end of the knowledge continuum (representing *idealism*) allow for individual construction of knowledge, personally or socially. Stimulus-response is a behaviorist approach, representing a "position that shares a learning theory with the didactic, expository approach, but makes no claims for the objective truth of what is learned" (Hein 1998, p. 29). The focus of stimulus-response is on the method where a specific action is followed by an anticipated response. Less emphasis is placed on the specific learning. In the museum, a hands-on exhibit may encourage children to complete a task such as filling a container to get positive feedback or a token reward. Filling the container [the stimulus] leads to a reward [the response], which fits this model.

This model, also known within the framework of behaviorism, is not necessarily an approach frequently used in museums. It is, however, praised for its strength as a methodology that supports the learning of special needs populations, young and old. In this case, the goal would be to reinforce behavior with some extrinsic reward, such as praise or a token, which in turn encourages the behavior to be repeated.

Constructivism, the final perspective in the model, falls within the quadrant defined by active learning while also recognizing knowledge as constructed within the individual. This perspective understands knowledge as unique to each individual based on prior knowledge, interests, cultural experiences, and other factors. For example, preschoolers visit an exhibition on early America that tells the story of children and play through toys from the era: hoops for rolling, spinning tops, whirligigs, and dolls made from corn husks and rags. Each child thinks about the toys displayed and the play scenarios that might ensue. The interpretation or understanding of play in early America would differ based on past experience and personal interests of each child, even though the exposure to the concepts in the museum would be similar for all children.

Research and theory about cognitive development point to the constructivist approach as the theory that most closely reflects the accepted views of museums and the early childhood field, and thus is the framework I emphasize in this volume. The constructivist perspective, held by theorists such as Dewey, Piaget, and Vygotsky, suggests that young children learn through interaction with their environment, which leads to construction of internal schemas or concepts representing their discoveries. With time and new encounters, children refine their schemas to reflect new information acquired through further experience.

There is broad interest in constructivist learning theory, particularly in informal learning environments such as museums, and especially for young learners. At the same time, educators in formal settings such as early childhood and elementary classrooms use strategies that are consistent with constructivist theory. In keeping with this current trend, the experts and theories selected for this volume fall within the framework of constructivist learning.

The Early Learning Model: A Constructivist Approach

Research and theory about children's learning is based primarily on the work of Jean Piaget and Lev Vygotsky, but includes perspectives from other theorists with similar ideas about the process of constructing knowledge. The child as an active participant in the learning process is central to theories about how children construct knowledge.

The Early Learning Model (ELM) defines the process of learning for young children and serves as an introduction to the concept. The model is further exploration of the constructivist quadrant as it relates to young children as learners.

ELM describes key elements that are essential in constructing knowledge. The process is dynamic and unending. ELM recognizes that young children *explore* their world, driven by an innate curiosity to learn and know. Exploration is an active process that contributes to meaning making and is in place at birth. Children *experience* their world in exploration, gathering information through their senses—sight, sound, taste, touch, and smell—and through social interactions. Children *conceptualize,*

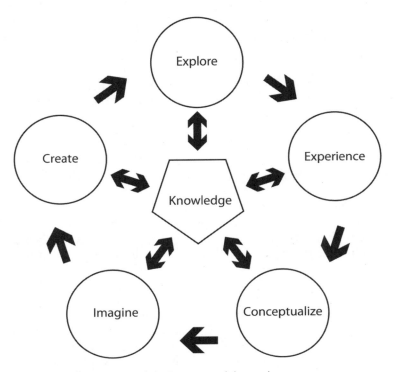

Figure 3.2. Early learning model. Courtesy of the author.

consciously and unconsciously, and create mental constructs from interactions with the environment. This internal process of conceptualization is critical to concept formation and constructing knowledge about the world. Children *imagine*—and represent a personal interpretation of reality—formulating ideas in play, narrative, and social interaction. Children *create*, expressing ideas through actions associated with play, language, and making, using personal knowledge of the world, the result of exploration, experience, conceptualizing, and imagining. As the process continues, children refine concepts based upon new experience. *Knowledge* is constructed throughout the process and reflects a constant rethinking or reimagining of concepts based upon new information acquired through experience.

ELM aligns with constructivist learning theory and is referenced in the themes discussed in this chapter: experience, play, ways of knowing, and motivation. ELM also serves as a framework for training museum docents and facilitators as described in chapters on best practice.

Thematic Approach to Learning Theory

Theme I: The Nature of Experience

Three-year-old Emma picked up pebbles along a path and examined them closely, feeling the shape and texture of each; sniffed a variety of flowers growing in the park, surprised that each had a different scent; watched the tiny bugs crawling on an old log to see how quickly they moved; and listened to birds in the trees and then imitated their sounds. Her visit to the park was driven by natural curiosity and marked by intentional exploration through her senses. She was experiencing nature and using her senses to build knowledge about the natural world.

Experience by its very nature suggests a connection to the senses—sight, sound, taste, touch, and smell—with each experience offering input to the learner by stimulation of one or more senses. In this context, experience exists in the concrete world rather than in an abstract form. Even so, there are some who would argue that an experience does not need to be concrete, but for the most part the term *experience* has concrete implications.

Children are by nature curious, a trait that leads to exploration and in turn experience. This interaction with the world is essential in the process of constructing knowledge. Emma expresses her curiosity regarding her surroundings during a family visit to the park and uses her senses to learn about her world. She actively explores her environment by noticing and examining objects along the path—pebbles, flowers, bugs, and birds—making personal discoveries about size, shape, pattern, texture, scent, sound, and movement. Curiosity, exploration, and experience are intertwined for Emma in her walk through the park.

Experience viewed as an encounter with the environment is a pathway to learning and takes center stage in the theories of many well-known educational philosophers. How do museum educators create experiences for young children that are meaningful and relevant? The answer to this question is grounded in the work of theorists and their insight regarding *experience*. For museum professionals, the study of theory should inform practice.

The nature of experience—the first theme—is embedded in the ideas associated with the discovery and constructivist quadrants of Hein's model. The discussion begins with John Dewey, the educational theorist most closely associated with the concept of experiential learning.

John Dewey (1859–1952), America's most influential educational philosopher, is best known for his belief in experiential learning. His theories reflect the basic tenets associated with constructivism. Dewey suggested that experience begins with an individual's interaction with the environment, but that contact with the environment is not sufficient for learning. According to Dewey, it is the reflection on the experience and response to the encounter—acting upon new information and applying previous knowledge—that produces knowledge rather than the contact itself (Dewey 1916).

Dewey valued problem-solving as an opportunity for engaging in quality mental processing, which contrasts with the more traditional method of seeking a specific answer. For example, when a young child discovers through trial and error that a triangular block is ill-suited for the base of a building, he gains valuable information about the nature of the block's shape and recognizes that it is unstable and unlikely to hold a larger structure. The discovery is far more effective as a means of learning than listening to verbal instruction reflecting the same ideas. It is the child's experience that leads to learning.

For Dewey, experience was not an end point but a stepping stone to further understanding. In "My Pedagogic Creed," Dewey (1897) states that "education must be conceived as a continuing reconstruction of experience," and suggests that each encounter contributes new information, leading to refinement of mental concepts and personal knowledge.

Counter to traditional schooling of his time (the early 1900s), Dewey emphasized a hands-on approach that placed the student at the center of learning. Even his thinking about the school's workspace is telling. In Dewey's search for furniture suitable for classrooms, he recounted a story about a furniture dealer who commented, "I am afraid we have not what you want. You want something at which the children may work: these are all for listening" (Dewey 1900, p. 48). Dewey's notion of school required space designed for active learning. It is possible to imagine what that might be—collaborative work areas, space for experimentation, places for authentic experiences, and possibly display areas—but certainly not the desk and chair options offered by the furniture dealer, which were far from ideal for experiential learning. Indeed, Dewey envisioned learning as an active process rather than the more traditional passive approach focused on listening and recitation.

Dewey also recognized that individuals draw upon their senses to explore and construct meaning about their world. And while this sensorial approach to learning is true for all learners, it is particularly true for young children. For Dewey, experiences in the concrete world offer opportunities to attach meaning to abstract ideas. His emphasis on "hands-on" as well as "minds-on" engagement of learners illustrates the point that experience is more than simply a physical interaction with the environment. His belief that learning emerges from mental interaction or cognitive engagement in the course of experience is accepted and embraced by many educators today.

Though hailed as a leader in American educational theory, Dewey was not the first to recognize the value of experience in learning. Johann Pestalozzi (1746–1827), a Swiss pedagogue, and Friedrich Froebel (1782–1852), the "Father of Kindergarten," developed *object lessons* for teaching young children, moving away from traditional practices and embracing a more active approach to learning. Pestalozzi believed in *"natural education—where the innate desire to learn is nourished and curiosity is unfettered"* and where "the tradition of interminable lectures followed by student recitation" is abandoned in favor of more active hands-on experiences (Brosterman 1997, p. 19). Froebel, German-born pedagogue and Pestalozzi's student, embraced the progressive ideas of his teacher and recognized the value of activity as essential to a child's learning. For Froebel, experience and play were intertwined and served as the foundation for Froebel's *kindergarten,* an idea that migrated across the globe and changed American education forever. This philosophy also informed the design of teaching materials intended to activate knowledge. Froebel gave careful thought to the development of his kindergarten materials and perceived them as *gifts*—yarn balls of different colors, blocks (sphere, cylinder, cube), pattern blocks of various shapes and color, and combinations of the objects—and believed that guided play would lead to learning. Pestalozzi and Froebel favored experiences embedded in nature and emphasized "learning by doing" (Brosterman 1997), a phrase later associated primarily with John Dewey and still considered one of the most effective techniques for early learning.

Lev Vygotsky (1896–1934), a Russian psychologist, offers yet another example of experience as fundamental to the process of learning. Although Vygotsky developed his theories in the first part of the twentieth century, they went unnoticed in America until the 1970s, and didn't gain prominence until the 1990s when his ideas of *socially mediated learning* and *scaffolding* became part of the education vernacular.

In his theory of learning, Vygotsky suggested that social interaction is perhaps the most critical element of constructing meaning. All learning comes from social experience where individuals, young and old alike, develop meaning through language and culture. A concept coined by Vygotsky as *the zone of proximal development (ZPD)* illustrates the significance of social interaction. ZPD begins with understanding baseline performance, defined by an individual's ability to be successful on an independent level; the upper limit indicates a threshold beyond which an individual lacks the ability to be successful regardless of support from others. Within the ZPD, the level of achievement increases with appropriate *scaffolding,* or support from a more knowledgeable peer or adult. For example, a three-year-old is capable of putting together a 10-piece puzzle without help or supervision (the baseline). With support or clues from a more knowledgeable partner, the child is able to successfully complete a 48-piece puzzle, a task that falls within ZPD. Support, or scaffolding, might be as simple as statements and questions intended to guide the process: *Let's look closely at the boat and find all of the puzzle pieces that are the same color as the boat. Did you notice that the edge of a puzzle is straight? Can you find puzzle pieces that have a straight edge to form the outside frame?* The amount of scaffolding will differ with each child and should reflect the child's needs and developmental level. Success with support is indicative of working in the ZPD. Tasks that are beyond the scope of a child's capacity, regardless of the amount of scaffolding, are outside the ZPD. For this three-year-old, a 500-piece jigsaw puzzle is likely to be beyond his abilities even with a capable partner guiding his efforts. This preschooler is learning through a social experience, gaining support through language that allows the child to function at a higher cognitive level. In this case, social experience is key.

Educators in all settings benefit from understanding Vygotsky's concept of scaffolding and serve children most effectively when challenging them within their ZPD. For many museum educators, the most difficult task is to quickly and accurately assess the knowledge and skills of a child or group to support their learning. This is a skill that for some is intuitive and for others learned through experience.

In *Thought and Language* ([1962] 1986), Vygotsky's discourse on learning continues with claims that experience becomes the teacher. "The sensory material and the word are both indispensable parts of concept formation" (Vygotsky [1962] 1986, p. 96–97). Lisbeth Dixon-Krauss (1996), author of *Vygotsky in the Classroom,* interprets the theorist's writings on concept formation, noting the pivotal role of a child's everyday experiences in the process.

> A child begins to label objects in her environment and groups them into random categories, or **heaps**. As her experiences in the world increase, she moves into thinking in **complexes**. During this stage, traits of objects are analyzed and concrete factual bonds or relationships among diverse objects are established through direct experience. (Dixon-Krauss 1996, p. 12)

Concept formation can be illustrated in an example of a child learning about the word *shoe*. Consider a young child with limited language, absorbing the meaning of words by listening and through visual context. Experience leads to meaning associated with words. The toddler learns that shoes, hats, and toys are things in her room (random categories), and later comes to understand that shoes and hats are worn (more refined categories). With experience, she soon discriminates based on distinguishing traits. Shoes are for feet, hats for heads (complexes). With experience, the toddler begins to understand that shoes can be sneakers, boots, or slippers and is able to analyze the specific features that distinguish one from another (more refined complexes). Experience, including social interaction, contributes to understanding.

Vygotsky's notion that all learning is socially mediated gained wide acclaim in education circles toward the latter part of the twentieth century and is still influential in the twenty-first century, contributing to how schools and museums think about engaging children and adults. It offers insight for educators as they think about their role in designing and implementing educational programs.

While Vygotsky was developing his ideas on socially mediated learning, Jean Piaget (1896–1980), a Swiss psychologist, was devoting his time to epistemology, the study of knowledge. Piaget's interest in how people learn led to intense study and observations of children and their acquisition of knowledge. His research on cognitive development and concept formation acknowledged the influence of sensory experience on learning.

In the context of gathering information through the senses, Piaget further described the process of constructing knowledge in terms of *assimilation* and *accommodation*. According to Piaget, as one encounters something new within the environment, the individual forms a mental construct, or *schema*, capturing the essence of the concept. With new encounters, relevant information about the concept is taken in or *assimilated* into what is known. Discrepancies between the existing schema and the new information lead to *accommodation*, a process refining or modifying the schema to reflect the more fully developed understanding of the concept. Mental constructs are really representations of the world developed through experience. For example, a young child drinks from a cup and mentally attaches the word *cup* to the object. With each new encounter with cups, a child gains new insight and understands that a cup can be made of many different types of materials—plastic, glass, metal—and can be different in shape, size, color, and design. A cup becomes more than the initial experience with the object, and as such, the mental construct evolves. A child begins to easily distinguish the difference between a parent's coffee cup and his own cup of juice, yet knows that both objects represent the concept of *cup*. This process of coming to know the meaning of cup happens over time and through multiple experiences with objects that have similar qualities associated with the term *cup*.

Piaget is known for his emphasis on sensory experience; he described the first phase of learning as the Sensory Motor Stage. A baby's earliest experiences are sensorial: feeling the warmth of a mother's touch to drifting off to sleep comforted by the gentle rocking of a grandparent and the soft sounds of a lullaby. As the baby becomes more independent, even playing on the floor, exploration begins with touching, tasting, and smelling each little treasure found.

While many have criticized Piaget's theory of developmental stages, few disagree with his notion that the senses—sight, sound, taste, touch, and smell—present a powerful entry point for acquiring information that contributes to concept formation and thus learning. The criticism alerts us to aspects of the theory that deserve greater attention. In Piaget's case, the chronological markers that define stages of development may not be as fixed as previously thought. Keeping this in mind is useful for museum educators as they plan for young children.

Piaget remains an influential leader in cognitive learning theory and provides insight into how learning occurs. His ideas are clearly positioned in constructivist theory and are valued by the early childhood community.

Like Dewey, Jerome Bruner (1915—) perceives experience as the foundation for learning and believes in the power of experience to transform the individual. Bruner emphasizes experimentation and discovery as critical elements of learning and sees experience as an opportunity to gather data as a means of problem-solving and answering questions about the workings of the world. Identification of similarities and differences becomes the foundation for categorizing and ultimately constructing meaning.

In *The Culture of Education* (1996), Bruner acknowledges Vygotsky's influence on his thinking, writing that "culture shapes the mind. . . . [I]t provides us with the toolkit by which we construct not only our worlds but our very conception of ourselves and our powers" (1996, p. x). The idea of culture includes the social interactions that contribute to the formation of ideas that define how the world works and what meaning is ascribed to places, events, and artifacts of everyday life. For Bruner, learning is a process that is an outcome of exploration and experience.

The Early Learning Model highlights critical actions that contribute to the construction of knowledge. Children *explore,* encouraged by natural curiosity, and *experience* the world through their senses. *Experience* leads to *conceptualization.* The first three elements of ELM are prominent in theories past and present. There is general agreement among experts in the constructivist camp that experience is an essential element of learning. While each theorist presents unique contributions to the field, there are common ideas that can help educators in schools and museums think about learning in their unique environments.

Theme II: Learning Through Play: A Child's Work

Jason's toy dinosaurs came to life through his pretend play. They roared, chased, and captured one another in their leafy habitat of the backyard. Jason was acting out his knowledge of dinosaurs and how they behaved based on his knowledge from children's books. On some days Jason arranged the dinosaurs in groups, based on common attributes that he noticed: red dinos near one bush, blue dinos by the pebbles, and green dinos on a mossy mound. As Jason realized that each dinosaur had a distinct shape, that information was integrated into his play and guided the process of sorting now by shape, but also was integrated into his understanding of dinosaurs more broadly. His actions were intricately linked to what he noticed in his play: that there were similarities and differences in his toy dinosaurs and that these features could be used to change how he interacted in play.

Much has been written about play as "a child's work" (Piaget [1951] 1962). Many perceive play as an instinctive behavior of young children, an idea confirmed by research in studies that show play as a concept that crosses cultural boundaries. It is recognized as a universal characteristic of human existence. Jason grounds his play in knowledge gleaned from prior experience, but also expands his understanding of dinosaurs through observations stemming from his experience of play, integrating new discoveries into his existing mental constructs.

Play comes in many forms and has diverse values. It can be planned or spontaneous, formal or informal, independent or social. Children test their ideas and develop greater understanding by trying on roles or acting out scenarios that they have experienced. Play is a means by which children make sense of their world and affords opportunities for physical, cognitive, and social development while setting the stage for collaboration and problem-solving. Because there is greater interest in the audience of young children, there is a need to understand play when creating effective programs and exhibitions.

Children's museums are designed with play in mind and offer exhibition space that encourages dramatic play: become the pastry chef at a bakery, join fellow construction workers to build a structure, step on the stage of a radio station as the new announcer, care for sick and injured animals as a veterinarian. Ideas are endless and are intended as opportunities for children to put into practice knowledge crafted through observation.

More traditional museums also have opportunities for play, but the strategy is not as common, nor is it fully developed. Museum educators can enrich children's experiences through innovative ideas that encourage play in galleries. In an art gallery, ask children to pose like a sculpture. Highlight imagination by inviting children into a world of pretend where they act out the story of a painting or imagine jumping into the painting. *What do you see? What is happening around you? What are you doing in the painting?* History, science, and cultural museums offer equally satisfying opportunities for pretend play as children become the paleontologist digging for fossils, astronauts preparing for lift-off, or a visitor to a past time. Props can add a different dimension, but are not essential for play. A child's imagination is powerful and requires little to be put in motion. By creating the scene and encouraging imagination, museums offer many possibilities for play in galleries. Jean Piaget ([1951] 1962) described play in various forms in *Play, Dreams, and Imitation in Childhood*. Imitation becomes a part of early play, but continues as children act seemingly without interest in reality while also attempting to recreate the roles and events from their experience, making an effort to conform to what is real grounded by their understanding. This tension, to replicate reality but at the same time to ignore reality, is evident in play scenarios.

Young children are learning about symbols and begin to integrate that concept into play. A child holds a block to her ear and initiates a conversation, imagining the block to be a cell phone. Costumes transform children into other characters. A young child puts on a tiara and becomes a princess; a baseball cap turns the child into a ball player. Make believe or pretend play is common in the lives of preschoolers.

Erik Erikson (1902–1994) perceived play as a critical element of social emotional development. Egocentrism—when a child sees his world through his personal point of view with little understanding that other perspectives exist—defines the early stages of life. Because a child perceives his world primarily from one point of view, there is a need for a safe place to explore conflict. Roleplay allows the child to work through conflict, trying out different interpretations of experiences while taking on the roles of others. According to Erikson, play also allows for a certain amount of autonomy whereby rules are set within the play, rather than by someone else. In play, a child is able to explore ideas and relationships without fear of being judged.

Lev Vygotsky saw play as an opportunity for a child to excel: "In play, it is as though he [the child] were a head taller than himself" (Vygotsky 1966, p. 102), in other words, the child demonstrates a maturity not demonstrated at other times. According to Vygotsky, in play a child adheres to rules inherent in the play, often behaving in ways that show greater self-control than ordinarily expected. For example, a child may resist eating candy if he is the cat in a play scenario, knowing that cats do not eat candy. In real life, a child may not be able to show the same level of restraint when candy is present.

Vygotsky (1966) wrote about play as "imagination in action" (p. 8), suggesting that children attach meaning to an object and act in accordance with that ordained meaning. For a child, a stick could be a horse or a block could be a car, but once identified, the object maintains the imagined properties associated with the original concept represented. Once the stick is a horse, it gallops but does not fly; the block representing a car moves quickly on pretend roads, but will not take on the attributes of a boat.

Vygotsky considered imagination and play as a means for children to make sense of the world. Pamela Krakowski described the power of imagination and play in the *Journal of Museum Education*. She referenced Vygotsky's concept of play, saying "In play children move from the reality of the here and now—the world that children experience through their senses—to the imagined world of what might be. They move from the actual to the possible, from the concrete to the abstract, from the *what is* to answering the question *what if*, and acting in ways that suggest *as if*" (Krakowski 2012, p. 55–56).

Vygotsky made connections between play and cognitive development, saying, "From the point of view of development, the fact of creating an imaginary situation can be regarded as a means of developing abstract thought" (Vygotsky 1966, p. 17). Vygotsky clearly recognized the role of play as integral to cognitive development; it is a topic that deserves attention by museum professionals as they venture into programming for younger audiences.

The museum field offers tangible examples of play, particularly in children's museums that design exhibitions around this concept. As an advocate for play, the Association of Children's Museums (ACM) notes that "In an increasingly complex world, children's museums provide a place where all children can learn through play" (ACM 2014b), and continues to demonstrate that museums can facilitate learning through exhibition design. As spaces created with children in mind, these institutions have an initial advantage over more traditional museums, but at the same time they provide insight that can be tapped by museum professionals for use in environments that are not solely developed for little ones. Thinking about play and its advantages for engaging young children is vital for any museum in the twenty-first century.

In ELM, play is essential to meaning making. Children base their play on mental constructs that represent their world and actively test theories in areas that are unclear. As children *conceptualize*, they reshape constructs and personal understanding based upon new experiences, a reflection of Piaget's theory of *assimilation* and *accommodation*. In this process, children *imagine* what might be based on what is known, using experiences and integrating the new with the old. Play is a powerful tool for constructing knowledge.

Theme III: Ways of Knowing

Four-year-olds in the pre-K class were embarking on a study of birds. In preparation for the unit, the children were asked to think about what they know about birds and then to be ready to share their knowledge the next day. Erika came to class with several drawings of birds, some based on robins that she had seen in her backyard and others reflecting her overall knowledge of birds; Lelia gave a lengthy explanation about the characteristics of birds, telling of her recent visit to the ornithology exhibit at a local museum; Stephen brought two feathers that he found at the park, encouraging his friends to use their sense of touch and smell to learn more about his specimens; Zoe eagerly shared her knowledge of birds by jumping to her feet, flapping her arms, and moving quickly around the room imitating a bird in flight; Gabe showed a photograph of his pet bird and smiled as he explained how the parakeet was almost like one of the family; Chyrstyna sang a song about birds that included bird calls of several species; Andrea recited a poem about birds that she had learned at home; and Karen asked each of her friends questions about birds during their presentations, learning through social interaction. In each case, these preschoolers were learning and sharing what they know about birds in a way that reflected a particular preference related to learning and knowing.

Learning is unique to each individual. Preferences, aptitudes, and attitudes toward learning affect how and what we learn. John Falk and Lynn Dierking capture this complexity in their Contextual Model of Learning (2013), where they suggest that learning is influenced by personal context, social context, and physical context. Learning is also related to time, which for museums means the process of learning begins before the visitor arrives at the museum and continues long after leaving the gallery space. This model shows learning as multifaceted and reinforces the concept that learning differs with individuals based upon a wide range of factors.

The concept of learning is not always easy to define or measure. In schools, learning is often measured by an individual's skill in language or in mathematical reasoning, both inextricably tied to symbolic understanding. Yet theories of learning are not limited to these capabilities and include a broader perspective, one that expands typical boundaries associated with intelligence. For some theorists, this concept is referenced as different ways of knowing. For museums, it makes sense to think about learning broadly. What does learning look like? What drives individuals in how they approach learning or express what they have learned?

Just as each child in the opening vignette expresses his or her knowledge of birds in a distinct way—describing, drawing, imitating—it is highly likely that in the learning process each child favors similar approaches to grappling with new ideas. Individuals possess personal interests, talents, and capacities for making meaning in the world, and learn or express ideas in different ways.

It makes sense that advocates for the arts are among those recognizing diverse ways of knowing. Eliott Eisner (1933–2014), an influential educator and leader in arts education, wrote of aesthetic modes of knowing that differed from the more typical conception of knowing. Eisner suggested that the world of aesthetics is of the heart and that engaging in the arts offers "experiential rewards of taking the journey" (Eisner 1985, p. 35) that differ from other modes of learning or knowing. Eisner viewed dance, musical composition and musical performance, visual artistry, and theatrical performance as opportunities for expressing ideas or developing deep understanding through the work of others. For young children, the array of experiences Eisner described is natural as a mode of learning and expressing ideas.

Howard Gardner (1943—), a developmental psychologist, extended America's standard approach to thinking about learning when he introduced his theory of multiple intelligences, a theory strongly embedded in experience and reflecting a belief in multiple ways of knowing. In *Frames of Mind: The Theory of Multiple Intelligences* (1983), Gardner argues that there is a wide range of cognitive abilities or intellectual strengths and initially identified seven ways of knowing—or intelligences—that arise from individual strengths and aptitudes: logical-mathematical, spatial, linguistic, bodily-kinesthetic, musical, interpersonal, and intrapersonal. Since that time, he has contemplated naturalistic and existentialist as possible intelligences. Multiple intelligences are acknowledged as ways of processing information and are considered independent of one another.

The intent of Gardner's theory is to broaden the concept of intelligence. Examples that fall outside of the typical boundaries of linguistic or mathematical thinking include knowing through physical aptitudes (bodily-kinesthetic), which recognizes individuals excelling in sports or dance; spatial abilities that acknowledge those who see and understand spatial relationships such as architects and designers; musical talent as a means of connecting with ideas and making sense of the world; and interpersonal capabilities that focus on knowing through relationships with others. All of these reflect different modes of knowing.

According to Gardner, "cognitive research ... documents the extent to which students possess different kinds of minds and therefore learn, remember, perform, and understand in different ways" (1991, p. 11). The idea that learning is not the same for everyone and that every individual has strengths that enable greater access to knowing and expressing ideas is central to the concept of multiple intelligences. It's easy to recognize individual preferences of the preschoolers in the vignette on birds.

Gardner's work initially received wide acclaim from educational institutions, from museums to schools, and continues to be included in conversations related to education. In some educational circles, Gardner's work led to reconstructing the practice of how teachers engage students. His theories are not without criticism, particularly from experts in psychology interested in understanding the construct of intelligence. While critics see multiple intelligences more simply as personality traits or talents, Gardner claims that each of the intelligences described in his theory is valuable as a way of knowing and believes that the idea of intelligence should not be limited to the more traditional framework of the past. Gardner's support for museums as environments conducive to different modes of learning makes his theories of interest to many in the museum field and encourages consideration of these ideas in relationship to programming and exhibit design.

Other theorists, including Jerome Bruner, have given thought to ways of knowing. Bruner, an early pioneer in learning theory, approached the topic not from the point of the individual strengths or differences, but from the perspective of different ways of representing in memory what is learned. According to Bruner (1966), ideas can be represented in memory in three modes: action-based (enactive representation), image-based (iconic representation), and language-based (symbolic representation). Action-based experience becomes encoded as part of muscle memory and is the earliest representation of experience. For example, riding a bike is encoded in muscle memory. Information can also be stored as mental images, a common practice for many individuals. A child sees the golden arches of

McDonald's and responds to the memory of that image and its associations: French fries. The most sophisticated mode of representation is symbolic, typically associated with language. Bruner suggested that the three modes are intertwined, and only loosely sequential, but typically appear in order of action, image, then language. Above all else, Bruner believes that children are active learners and that education should be viewed as an opportunity to teach abstract thinking and problem-solving.

Different ways of knowing acknowledges the individuality of learning. Inherent in ELM is the role of the individual to construct knowledge. Children *conceptualize*, forming internal constructs based upon exploration and experience. They *imagine* possibilities that emerge from constructs shaped in conceptualization. Important to constructing knowledge is the ability to imagine something new. Children ultimately *create*—in play, through language, or in making—expressing ideas that come from a unique understanding of the world, crafted from prior knowledge, interests, and social interactions. Understanding that every child's thoughts are distinctive is fundamental to meaning making.

Theme IV: Motivation and Learning

> Henry was a preschooler intrigued by baseball, every aspect of the game. Through visits to the Nationals ballpark and conversations with family members, he learned the rules of the game, positions and names of players, and statistics reflecting their success. Henry's love of baseball led to a greater understanding of mathematics as his father explained some of the statistics associated with the game. It also led to a desire to learn to read so that he could follow baseball and his favorite players in the newspaper. His interest in the sport was embedded in his conversations as well as in his worldview. If something related to baseball, there was no need to convince Henry to take part or invest in the experience. His love of the sport was clearly a driving force in his life.

Many theorists examine motivation in learning. The concept of motivation is perceived as a force that creates desire and interest toward pursuit of a specific goal or behavior, a force that can emerge from internal or external factors. For museums, as for schools, learning is tied to the engagement of the individual, which in turn reflects motivation.

The opening vignette for this section clearly identifies the motivational force that drives Henry's actions. His passion for the sport of baseball supersedes almost any other activity in life, with the exception of time with his family. It might even be said that motivation allows Henry to perform at a level higher than expected, a feat not dissimilar to Vygotsky's notion of a child at play. For Henry, there was a reason to attend to new information. And whether mastering mathematical skills or tackling challenging words in the newspaper, Henry's enthusiasm for baseball drove his actions and led to accomplishments.

Dewey believed that the most appropriate method for educating a child is one that reflects a child's interests. In "My Pedagogic Creed," Dewey (1897) suggests "only through the continual and sympathetic observation of childhood interests can the adult enter a child's life and see what it is ready for, and upon what material it could work most readily and fruitfully" (p. 15). These interests are a natural extension of the child and offer an entry point for determining curriculum or educational experiences. For Dewey, the intellectual curiosity of the child forms the basis for all learning. Evidence of this curiosity occurs at the earliest stages of life.

Dewey also made a connection between school and society, suggesting that real-world occupations are the key. An "occupation supplies the child with genuine motive; it gives him experience at first hand; it brings him into contact with realities" (Dewey, 1900, p. 37). It is difficult to separate Dewey's belief in active learning associated with the real world and a child's motivation to learn. Dewey showed great respect for the child in his desire to honor individual interests and authentic learning experiences.

Bruner concurred with Dewey in thinking that interest in the subject matter serves as a powerful stimulus for learning. In *The Process of Education: A Landmark in Educational Theory*, Bruner (1960) suggests that "arousing the child's interest in the world of ideas" is essential for education and is best accomplished through the selection of interesting material, providing a sense of discovery, and framing the experience in a manner that speaks to the developmental level of the child. Bruner (1960) further suggests that "The best way to create interest in a subject is to render it worth knowing, which means to make the knowledge gained usable in one's thinking and beyond the situation in which the learning has occurred" (p. 31).

The real focus for educators is how to make the experience relevant and meaningful for young learners. Think about what is happening in your community, and design an experience around that event. If a new bridge is under construction, look for opportunities to explore the concept of bridges. Photographs of bridges in art, history, or science museums can be connected to building structures of bridges in the galleries. Of course, document the children's work with digital images and then display the photographs. If the community is planting flowers or gardens in common areas, children can explore the idea of planting by incorporating outdoor garden spaces in science centers or children's museums. If a new art installation is planned for the city, invite the artist to create collaborative art with visitors during a Family Day. Interviewing preschoolers and kindergartners to find out what's important in their world might also lead to suggestions for experiences in museums. The goal is to reach children through relevant and meaningful experiences.

Abraham Maslow (1908–1970) is known for a humanistic approach to understanding motivation. He envisioned learning in direct response to

Self-Actualization
Pursue talent, creativity, fulfillment

Self-Esteem
Achievement, Mastery, Recognition

Belonging
Friends, Family, Community

Safety
Security, Shelter

Physiological
Food, Water, Warmth

Figure 3.3. Maslow's Hierarchy of Needs.

motivation where personal circumstance shapes actions. Maslow's model is a hierarchical construct where the base of the pyramid, or most elemental level, reflects physiological needs followed by the need to feel safe and secure, and then a sense of belonging or love. The next level centers around self-esteem and respect for self and others. The highest point of the pyramid is described as self-actualization, where problem-solving, open-mindedness, creativity, and morality are evident. At each level, individuals are motivated by a set of needs or circumstances where those needs must be met before an individual can move to a higher level. In this model, motivation is closely tied to an individual's circumstances.

Maslow's description and prioritization of needs offers a point of departure for museum educators interested in the motivation of children and families visiting their museums. Which of the needs can be met by the museum? How can museums create a sense of comfort and belonging in the museum? What types of activities might encourage achievement or mastery, even though children will not be reaching those goals at an early age? This tool for understanding motivation might prove useful in thinking about programs at the museum.

Many museum professionals draw from another thought leader on motivation, Mihaly Csikszentmihalyi (1934–), a Hungarian psychologist educated at the University of Chicago. In his research, Csikszentmihalyi defines motivation as intrinsic (something that comes from an internal desire) or extrinsic (an external motivator such as a reward or some other incentive). His studies suggest that intrinsically motivated individuals are more likely to establish goals and pursue challenges.

Csikszentmihalyi and Hermanson discuss the critical link between intrinsic motivation and interest in their 1999 article *Intrinsic Motivation in Museums: Why Does One Want to Learn?* "The first step in the process of intrinsically motivated learning suggests that the museum exhibit must capture the visitors' curiosity" (Csikszentmihalyi and Hermanson 1999, p. 153). The authors indicate that once curiosity is aroused, interest must be sustained for learning to take place.

In the context of his study of motivation, Csikszentmihalyi coined the term *flow,* which he associates with an activity that is intrinsically motivated. As an individual develops competence—for example, as a musician, a tennis player, a lecturer—the actions associated with the task become second nature. A high degree of concentration and knowledge of the action leads to anticipation of the next step because the individual knows what is likely to happen. At the same time, feedback from actions allows for minor adjustments, but the overall experience is one of *flow,* which is a balance of challenge and skills. Expertise is at such a high level that the action becomes automatic. The feeling associated with the experience is rewarding and drives future interest to continue to exceed previous accomplishments. Think about Michael Jordan in his prime, or Yo-Yo Ma as he creates extraordinary music: both individuals have certainly experienced flow in their areas of expertise.

And although flow is most often associated with those who excel in some specific activity, the flow experience is something that others enjoy as well. For children, flow may occur when a child is deeply absorbed in an activity to the point of being oblivious to his surroundings. This might happen in block play or propelling oneself through the air on a swing. The activity absorbs the mind and spirit.

Csikszentmihalyi's research on motivation as a significant factor in the learning process is useful for educators as they think about learning in museums. ELM recognizes that children *explore* based on curiosity and learn through *experience.* Personal interests developed in the context of experience lead to new pursuits and further learning. Interest also drives a child's ability to *imagine* and *create,* serving as a motivating force.

Conclusion

Learning is a complex process that can be examined in many ways. Hein's model offers educators a visual explanation of the complexity of learning. The individual nature of learning and the complex nature of the process are also evident in ELM, situated in a constructivist approach to learning.

Educational theorists study learning as a process and develop explanations that describe the interaction of factors associated with learning. There are some who see theories as fixed, yet in truth they are dynamic and continue to be refined as scholars contemplate ideas and glean new insights.

As educators and other professionals representing museums become more engaged in serving younger audiences, knowledge of theory and how the ideas support practice is increasingly important. Intuition about how young children learn is not sufficient for creating enriching, educational learning environments and programs, but rather is a complementary force that will drive effective practice.

A wonderful example that demonstrates the connection between theory and practice is David Rockwell's Imagination Playground at the National Building Museum in Washington, DC. In this unique gallery space designed for family engagement, children and adults explore concepts of construction through play with large, blue foam blocks. The experience engages children through their senses, particularly the kinesthetic sense, and encourages use of imagination. Play encourages social interaction with peers and family members. Tapping into children's interest in building and natural inclination to play aligns with what we know about how children learn.

This brief overview of educational theory and significant thinkers in the field merely touches the surface; it offers a brief introduction to some of the basic characteristics of learning by categorizing them by theme. Theorists' views on experience, play, ways of knowing, and motivation for learning begin to form a baseline of knowledge and can be exceedingly helpful for individuals as they plan and interact with young children in classrooms and museum settings.

Shaping Programs that Engage Children in Constructing Meaning

CHAPTER FOUR

The Early Childhood Classroom and Museum Learning

"The wider the range of possibilities we offer children, the more intense will be their motivations and the richer their experiences. We must widen the range of topics and goals, the types of situations we offer and their degree of structure, the kinds and combinations of resources and materials, and the possible interactions with things, peers, and adults."
—*Loris Malaguzzi, Reggio Emilia*

Introduction

Learning is a part of everyday life for young children and certainly is not limited to one specific place. It happens formally in classrooms and informally at home, at the grocery store, or when playing with friends in the neighborhood. The natural interests and impulses of children along with a sense of curiosity remain intact regardless of where they are. There really are few boundaries when it comes to places of learning.

The early childhood classroom is often associated with learning and places an emphasis on supporting children's cognitive, physical, social, and emotional growth. For that reason it makes sense to take a closer look at the experience of children in classrooms as a window into the learning process. In these specially designed spaces, it is possible to gather ideas applicable to museum settings.

There are many different early childhood models and programs, some extraordinary and some quite ordinary; some reflect excellence, while others can at best be described as mediocre. For the purposes of this book, our interest is in quality programs grounded in best practice as perceived by the early childhood field. The insights gleaned from an analysis of effective methodologies have the potential to inform practice and decision-making for museum professionals as they enter or seek to refine their efforts in early learning.

A few models worthy of discussion include the Montessori Method, the Reggio Emilia model, and the High Scope approach, as well as several other unique practices that deserve recognition. Some models have greater recognition than others, just as certain practices are better known within

Engaging Young Children in Museums, by Sharon E. Shaffer, 71–87. © 2015 Left Coast Press, Inc. All rights reserved.

the field. Practices that are prominent in high-quality programs include inquiry-based learning, project-based exploration, arts-rich learning, and museum-based experiences. As we look at the models, it is also helpful to consider evaluation criteria.

The Early Childhood Classroom

Today's dialogue about learning includes discussion of two distinct ways to categorize the experience: formal and informal learning. Formal learning is typically associated with schools, while informal learning is perceived in the context of social or cultural experiences represented by museums and libraries. Formal learning is also understood as more structured and has accountability for learning outcomes, whereas informal learning is viewed through the lens of personal choice without any responsibility for achieving specific goals.

Although early childhood education falls within the realm of formal learning, classrooms are actually a mix of methodologies that reflect the formal and the informal. Most programs are a blend of structured experiences—circle time, morning meeting, or story time—and unstructured activities where choice of activity is the promise, even though teachers may at times limit the choices to a few distinct options.

The array of activities and the diversity in quality of programs in America's early childhood classrooms is stunning, ranging from untrained teachers with meager resources to privileged schools touted as stepping stones to the Ivy League. Even with this range of possibilities there are some constants that represent the vast majority of programs or, at the very least, the typical early childhood program.

A snapshot of a typical early childhood classroom captures the nature of young children as learners: it is a place of high energy, eager participation, and self-expression. A defining feature of most preschool classrooms is activity. Children engage in imaginative play, reading books, block building, singing, and art making. There usually are opportunities for hands-on discovery and exploration using materials such as attribute blocks, sorting objects, and natural specimens like shells, leaves, and plants. For most children, physical movement often trumps more passive experience as a means of interacting with the environment.

Each activity is typically coupled with a constant narration by the individual child, referred to by Vygotsky ([1962] 1986) as *egocentric speech*. When engaged in complex or challenging activities, children often direct their own behavior by verbalizing the sequence of actions required. Based on what we know about children and their unique preferences, it's easy to understand why preschool classrooms are filled with the sounds of activity.

The best programs offer rich experiences for children with opportunities for exploration, experimentation, and discovery. Teachers serve as facilitators, at times modeling and more frequently encouraging interactions with interesting objects and child-friendly materials. Children are naturally drawn to unusual or thought-provoking objects, from the tiniest insect curling into a ball on the sidewalk to a decorative kitchen timer shaped like a chicken, always with a natural curiosity for the how and why of the workings of their world. Museums, with collections of unusual and captivating objects, are well equipped to tap into this natural curiosity.

Each model has distinct characteristics, and yet there is a common bond: respect for the child and the process of learning. A closer look at some of the early childhood models sets the stage for sharing knowledge across boundaries with the potential of bringing about change and ultimately transforming old notions of museums and the audiences they serve.

Models in Early Learning

The Montessori Method

The Montessori Method represents the work of Maria Montessori (1870–1952), the first female physician in Italy. Her deeply held belief in the child as the center of learning led to Montessori's creation of a real-life laboratory, Casa del Bambini, dedicated to teaching preschool children.

Her unique educational approach recognized the early years, from birth through age six, as the *stage of the absorbent mind* and a time when children were more sensitive to learning. Within the Montessori model, when a child "is given the freedom to explore, examine, experiment, and interact with the multitude of objects and situations in his environment, the child is stimulated and energized, and gains a sense of power in a period of literal self-creation" (Cooney et al. 1993, p. 152).

According to Montessori, an environment that reflects natural beauty entices a child to explore and discover, shaping learning through personal interaction. Natural woods and materials make up the child-centered space, where furniture and teaching objects are crafted specifically for children, a novelty in Montessori's time. The learning environment is thoughtfully prepared to allow each child to work independently and make personal choices as to how to spend his time.

Montessori believed that children are innately attentive to their surroundings and that experiencing the world through the senses should be embodied in educational practice. This engagement, referred to by Montessori as *concentration* (Hyson 2008), offers a rationale for encouraging independent activity and acknowledges that children become absorbed in their experimentation with materials in their surroundings. Montessori recognized the value of preparing the environment to include objects that will capture a child's attention and pique interest so that exploration is the natural outcome (Cooney et al. 1993). Montessori designed activities to emphasize sensory experiences, from comparing textures to identification of sounds, and to encourage children to master materials through self-directed learning.

Montessori materials are designed specifically for independent work in the classroom and allow for self-correction. Wooden cylinders of increasing diameter fit precisely into a base ordered from the smallest cylinder to the largest. The pink tower is a set of stacking blocks that when stacked from the largest to the smallest create a tower. Sandpaper numerals introduce the shape as a visual and tactile experience to reinforce the concept through multiple senses. Single-shape puzzles are perfect for the youngest Montessori children. Materials are objects of beauty and purpose that encourage active learning.

The teacher's role is as facilitator, sometimes as observer, and always as one who respects the individual nature of the child. Children are introduced to new materials through teacher-led demonstrations, often with little or no explanation. Educators assess the development of each child through observations of a child's interactions with classroom materials, noticing mastery of specific tasks and offering additional practice and encouragement to further develop other skills. This interaction is a carefully constructed balance of providing independence for the child while offering support and guidance as needed. Respect for the development of the child—physical, social, emotional, and cognitive domains—underlies all aspects of the Montessori Method along with the belief that children experience an intrinsic joy in learning that should be valued.

Contemporary programs based on Maria Montessori's methods vary in implementation, but typically retain the basic values defined by her pioneering efforts. As one approach to early learning, the Montessori Method honors the child, encourages self-directed learning, engages the senses, and recognizes the innate curiosity of the child.

> Three-year-old Emma watched intently as her Montessori teacher presented the deconstruction and reconstruction of the Pink Tower, a set of 10 deeply pink wooden blocks that grow increasingly larger in size. Her teacher stacked the blocks with graceful, precise movements that Emma will strive to emulate. After observing the modeling by her teacher, Emma was invited to build the tower herself. Over time and through concentration, Emma gained mastery of this exercise.
>
> Within the Montessori experience, children develop mastery through a process of experimentation and practice. After Emma becomes a master Pink Tower builder and internalizes the sensorial experience of size, she will be given language of smallest and largest. The totality of the Pink Tower exercise involves

Figure 4.1. Building a tower from largest to smallest. Photo by Stephen Shaffer.

building concentration, a sense of order, independence, and a reverence for work. In the Montessori approach to learning, words are but a distraction for the young child and unnecessary to convey deep meaning. (Laura Gottfried, Principal, EAC Montessori School of Ithaca; personal communication)

Reggio Emilia Approach

In the late 1940s in Reggio Emilia, Italy, Loris Malaguzzi (1920–1994) developed an educational approach for young children in collaboration with parents in surrounding villages. Educational practices of the time were influenced by Froebel's kindergarten, the work of Maria Montessori, the research of Jean Piaget, and the progressive ideas of John Dewey, among others (Edwards et al. 2012), which in turn informed the newly developing school in Reggio Emilia. Today, the progressive child-centered program is recognized around the world as a model for early childhood education and is known for its emphasis on an emergent, project-based curriculum where children's interests are the impetus for areas of study. A unique characteristic of the Reggio Emilia Approach is recognition of myriad opportunities for self-expression.

The Reggio Emilia experience fosters children's intellectual development through a systematic focus on symbolic representation. Young children are encouraged to explore their environment and express themselves through multiple paths and all their "languages" including the expressive, communicative, symbolic, ethical, metaphorical, logical, imaginative, and relational. (Reggio Children 2010, p. 4)

The forces influencing the formation of Reggio Emilia schools contributed to the underlying principles of and belief in an active, dynamic environment that creates a place of shared relationships among children, parents, and teachers. Respect is an honored practice, and families have a place of privilege as equal members of the school community. This is more than a series of individual relationships, but a culture of community.

Children shape the school experience (Edwards et al. 2012). Teachers work collaboratively to build units of study around the ideas of children, using evolving interests as a source of inspiration for collective projects. Observation, exploration, discovery, and questioning are integral to this learning process. This notion of *emergent curriculum*—units of study or lessons that arise from student interest—is now commonplace in many early childhood programs because of the Reggio Emilia model.

Learning is not limited to classrooms, but also extends to outdoor environments. Most programs modeled on Reggio Emilia schools also include a children's workshop or *atelier*, designed as a "school studio and laboratory" created "for manipulating or experimenting with separate or combined visual languages" (Edwards et al. 2012, p. 41) for the purpose of encouraging active exploration. Children work independently or with classmates using clay, paint, and materials from nature in project work related to topics of study. This child-centered focus, where children make meaning based on their interactions with others and their environment, remains at the heart of the Reggio Emilia model.

Documentation of student work is a hallmark of the Reggio Emilia Approach. Through photographs, written text, student work, and related objects, projects are documented for review by students, parents, teachers, and community members. For example, one group of preschoolers learned of a local bridge in disrepair that was to be replaced with a more modern structure. This piqued the interest of the children and became the impetus for a collaborative project where the children, with support and guidance by teachers, visited different bridges in the area, read books about design and construction of these structures, and created small models of wooden bridges based on research. A display of the handmade models along with descriptions served as documentation of the learning process. Included in the documentation were children's drawings showing intricate patterns seen in area bridges and photographs from the project study. Classroom photographs captured interactions between a visiting engineer and children as they discussed vital aspects of designing a bridge. All of this became part of the project documentation.

This process reflects a high level of respect for student learning and is crafted with great care and attention. Documentation makes the process visible and creates a permanent record of the work that can be revisited during future units of study.

The *hundred languages of children,* a phrase associated with the Reggio Emilia model, refers to the many ways that children construct meaning and express ideas, from song and dance to words and art making. Reggio Emilia applauds this great diversity in how children understand their world and encourages an open mind in education that allows this creativity to flourish.

> *Opal School, inspired by the Reggio Emilia model, is abuzz with thinking about learning. In the last few weeks, children in Preschool have discovered, encountered and collected many different types of seeds: within beans pods brought from a child's garden, in dissecting the fruit during lunch, stuck to the legs of our pants after a hike, on a trail below a tree, on the stem of a picked dandelion...*
>
> *The spark the children have about exploring seeds is contagious. They have been looking closely, testing, theorizing and exploring. Through observing them work and talking with them as they explore, we have taken note of the many questions they are asking through investigation:*
>
> - *What do I notice about the outside of the seed?... [W]hy does it make noise when I shake it?*
> - *How many beans inside a pod? What is a pod?*
> - *Do beans have belly buttons, too? Are they babies?*
> - *Can they fly? Why?*
> - *The seed is following me.... Can a seed like me?* (Wolfe 2012; used with permission of Portland Children's Museum Center for Learning)

High Scope

High Scope is one example of a research-based early childhood curriculum known for its child-centered approach to teaching and learning. It grew from the Perry Preschool Study initiated in 1968 to compare different early childhood methodologies and identify the long-term impact on individuals. The study analyzed three early childhood approaches: direct instruction, play-based learning, and the High Scope initiative. The outcomes were revolutionary at the time and added a dimension to the debate among early childhood educators about best practice.

The High Scope curriculum is structured around the concept of *active participatory learning,* a process designed with the child as a co-creator in constructing meaning about his world. An underlying principle of the program seeks authentic work initiated by the child, which typically is evident in a child's actions. In this natural approach to learning children observe, explore, experiment, compare, predict, analyze, and communicate their ideas and findings. Observation leads to recognition of similarities and differences, a basis for sorting, ordering, and classifying objects based on specific characteristics or attributes. For example, a child collects leaves, nuts, seeds, and pebbles on a nature walk then returns to the classroom to examine his treasures. The child examines his collection and then begins to sort his objects into piles separating the objects by category: leaves, nuts, seeds, pebbles. As children gain experience in observation and analysis of everyday life, they develop a comfort with higher-order thinking and become more confident in their capacity to learn.

This early childhood methodology is based on a set of principles about children and how they learn, influenced by Piaget's theory of development (Hyson 2008). Key to the approach is the founders' belief in the individuality of each child and the role of the teacher as a facilitator supporting intellectual and social growth. Children's interests and preferences for learning become central to the learning process, in which preschoolers have choice or ownership for their activities within a specific unit of study.

The High Scope curriculum is structured around an approach that reflects these principles and places an emphasis on fostering habits of mind that value curiosity, problem solving, creativity, persistence, and independence. The program introduces children to a unique routine for learning (plan-do-review) where children are encouraged to plan (think ahead to what they want to accomplish), do (actively pursue their goals), and review (reflect on the outcome of their actions with others).

The curriculum encompasses multiple disciplines—language arts, science, social studies, mathematics, and creative arts—and emphasizes underlying concepts rather than specific skills. "The curriculum is organized around key developmental indicators (formerly known as *key experiences*); active learning promotes understanding of these and other concepts" (Hyson 2008, p. 74).

Within creative arts—music, movement, pretend play, visual arts—children express ideas and feelings about their world through singing, dancing, performing, and appreciating art, experiences that contribute to artistic and creative development. Interestingly, art is more than art making or craft, but extends to appreciating the creations of others in venues within the community. While the arts are valued for their intrinsic worth, there is an understanding that other skills are developed through artistic experiences. Children learn sequencing, develop new vocabulary, represent ideas in diverse ways, and expand social awareness through collaborative interplay.

The aims of High Scope are to engage children actively in the learning process and to nurture dispositions that remain instrumental in constructing meaning about the world in the future. The process of learning addresses all domains of learning—social, emotional, physical, and cognitive—where the development of the whole child is valued.

Educational Practices

The Project Approach

The concept of project-based learning is not new, but emerges from theoretical constructs that date back to the time of Aristotle and his belief in learning by doing. From Aristotle to John Dewey and educational leaders in the twenty-first century, there have been advocates for an approach to learning that is an outcome of active engagement with the environment. Early references to this practice can be found in John Dewey's laboratory school at the University of Chicago, where Dewey encouraged student projects requiring mental activity, such as making judgments and integrating ideas through a process of "seeking, finding, using, organizing, digesting, and assimilating information" (Marlowe and Page 2005, p. 11). Dewey believed that this type of activity would create habits of mind as well as build knowledge that would serve future learning (Tanner 1997).

The idea of project-based learning—a study that involves in-depth, active exploration of a topic—is a practice visible in specific models like Reggio Emilia and is also commonly accepted in early childhood education. Children investigate and solve problems through a collaborative process. The integrity with which the project study is pursued differs across programs, much like the quality of experiences.

A proponent of the project approach and a strong advocate for the value of deep exploration of concepts is Dr. Lilian Katz, a graduate of Stanford University and an international leader in early childhood education. Her work in project-based learning began in 1970 and continues today, setting her apart from others as an expert in the field with particular interest in engaging young children in projects. Katz is known for her many contributions to early childhood journals and is recognized internationally for her work on project-based learning. *Young Investigators: The Project Approach in the Early Years* (Helm and Katz 2001) offers a detailed account of project-based learning.

A primary goal of the project approach is to engage students in meaningful exploration that leads to in-depth understanding of concepts and their context. This approach begins with thought-provoking questions generated by children and ultimately taps into the natural curiosity inherent in children to motivate complex and thoughtful study leading to intellectual growth.

Topics for study arise naturally from children's interests or emerge from experiences related to the curriculum. Questions often stimulate a desire to learn more about a topic. For example, preschoolers on a walk around the neighborhood notice that the nearby park is being transformed with new gardens filled with flowers and other types of plants. The children wonder about the plants, where they come from, and who is responsible for taking care of the new gardens. This becomes the impetus for a project.

79

The introductory phase of the study is identifying questions, making possible connections to curriculum, and defining introductory activities to begin examination of the topic. Analysis of student understanding of concepts coupled with targeted questions that students wish to investigate set the stage for the second phase of the project study. Investigation through hands-on activities, field trips, and interviews with experts provides children with deeper understanding and insight into the content of the study. Reflection is the final phase and a time of debriefing and reassessing achievement of goals and next steps.

The project approach places the child at the center of learning and establishes an environment in which questioning, experimentation, and meaning making are fostered. Learning is authentic and originates from within the child. The ultimate goal is to seek deeper understanding of the world through personal and collaborative exploration.

Inquiry Approach

Far from new, inquiry has its origins in ancient Greece in the teachings of Socrates, a man known for his contributions to philosophy and education. Today's inquiry is grounded in open-ended questioning similar to the Socratic Method, but differs in that current strategy is more broadly applied across education to seek understanding about objects, concepts, and experiences, rather than limited to Socrates' focus on moral issues.

To understand Socrates' pedagogical practice is to gain insight into the underlying principles of today's thinking about inquiry. Socrates valued dialogue as a means of reaching new understandings through a process of shared experience between individuals. In the Socratic Method, "the teacher, or leader of the dialogue, asks probing questions in an effort to expose the values and beliefs which frame and support the thoughts and statements of the participants in the inquiry. The students ask questions as well, both of the teachers and each other" (Reich 2003, p. 1). Teacher and student have a shared responsibility for moving the dialogue forward through a process of questioning.

Through open-ended questions, ideas or issues are deconstructed to gain new insight into values and myriad perspectives that open one's mind and achieve new understanding. This way of thinking about teaching and learning is as valuable today as it was 2,500 years ago.

In the early childhood classroom, inquiry begins with open-ended questions that frame learning as a process for seeking information through dialogue and investigation. When a child brings a seed pod into the classroom and asks questions about the object, teachers dedicated to inquiry open a conversation that nurtures observation and exploration rather than simply providing the answers. This way of thinking mirrors Dewey's belief that knowledge is constructed in the process of experience or interaction with the environment, and that an individual cannot truly know without meaningful action and reflection.

Inquiry is not specific to one early childhood model, but is embedded in programs representing diverse learning experiences. It is a way of thinking about learning that is child-centered and discovery-based, a common trait for programs using this methodology.

It is common for educators interested in nurturing scientific thinking to favor inquiry and see it as a cornerstone for the study of science. Many consider the creation of a culture of inquiry a hallmark of best practice. As children interact with their environments, they acquire knowledge of scientific concepts and form ideas about the world.

Through informal and formal experiences, teachers guide learning using open-ended questions and support children as they observe, investigate, experiment, collect data, reflect on their practice, communicate findings, and construct meaningful explanations in this process of learning (Chalufour and Worth 2004).

Leaders advocating the study of science for young children produce educational materials that make inquiry-based learning accessible for classroom teachers and children. *Surrounded by Science* (Fenichel and Schweingruber 2010), which is based on the National Research Council study *Learning Science in Informal Environments: People, Places, and Pursuits* (Bell et al. 2009), provides case studies, illustrative examples, and probing questions for practitioners, making valuable research accessible (Fenichel and Schweingruber 2010).

Although inquiry is perceived in different ways by different individuals, it is important to note that at its base inquiry is a process that aims to extract meaning from experience (Audet 2005). The goal of an inquiry model is to create a culture of learning steeped in actively seeking knowledge through a process of exploration and questioning.

To begin a nature study, the four-year-olds collect leaves from the park and playground, later to examine their collections prior to a class discussion. The teacher encourages the preschoolers to look closely at one large multi-colored leaf. *What do you notice about this leaf?* Children share their observations: *it's big; it has lots of colors on it; there are points on the leaf; it crumbles if you aren't careful; it is scratchy; it falls slowly when I drop it.* With each observation, the teacher restates the child's response and asks a related question to extend the thinking. *Are all leaves the same size and how do you know?* One child gathers five other leaves from the collection and compares the large multi-colored leaf with the smaller varieties collected by the class. The children also ask questions inspired by the objects. *Why are the leaves different shapes?* The teacher in turn responds with a question to encourage critical thinking. *Are all trees the same?* The teacher encourages contemplation of the question and how it might relate to leaves of different shapes. Other questions will continue to engage the children in their exploration of leaves. *Can you tell us more about the shape of each leaf?* The child who initially focused on the pointy aspect of the leaf traces the exterior edge of the large leaf, noting the points and then realizes that there are also curved edges in the leaf. With encouragement to look more closely at the leaf, new discoveries add to the initial impression. The children are learning to show evidence that confirms their conclusions. With each child's observation, the teacher encourages further thought through open-ended questions.

Arts-rich Learning

Education through the arts brings an expressive quality to learning that taps into the human spirit. Programs rich in music, creative movement, dance, visual art experiences, or dramatic performance reflect an arts-rich learning environment. Children experience their world through modalities other than the linguistic mode that permeates classrooms and are learning by engaging their senses.

While most early childhood programs would claim a connection to the arts, a program truly dedicated to the arts is defined by experiences that fall within areas recognized as creative and expressive endeavors, immersing students in the art form. For example, there are schools where the creative experience of music, creative and rhythmic movement, and dance are the core of the program. The culture of the school reflects a broad commitment to music and values this type of activity for its benefits to students. It surpasses the typical singing and art making that is identified with early childhood education.

Arts integration is another approach to learning that differs from immersive arts experience emphasizing one or several specific art forms. Arts integration is broader and sees that content and art disciplines offer parallel and complementary learning opportunities in which understanding in each distinct discipline is achieved by involving specific content with arts instruction in tandem. The Kennedy Center in Washington, DC, offers a comprehensive definition of arts integration as "an approach to teaching students in which students construct and demonstrate understanding through an art form. Students engage in a creative process which connects an art form and another subject area and meets evolving objectives in both" (Silverstein and Layne 2010).

In a kindergarten class exploring the mathematical concept of pattern, listening to folk songs with repeating patterns or learning a simple dance that repeats a series of steps throughout sets the stage for a class discussion about patterns and how they are a part of our world. Arts integration embeds the arts in all aspects of learning so that children develop deeper understanding of concepts through arts-rich experiences, but also develop skills and knowledge about the art form itself.

Museum-based Approach

The museum-based approach is used to engage children in constructing meaning through objects and collections. The Smithsonian Early Enrichment Center (SEEC) is the Smithsonian Institution's model lab school where children aged six and younger explore concepts and learn about the world through the rich collection of natural specimens, cultural artifacts, and works of art housed in the museum complex. This object-based approach is steeped in inquiry and project-based learning and is rich in the arts.

Museums are repositories for objects that tell stories of our world, past and present, near and far. The children learn that each object tells a story and represents something in the real world. When visiting the Peddler's Cart at the National Museum of American History, SEEC preschoolers compare old-fashioned brooms, pails, a butter churn, and ladles on the cart with today's version of kitchen utensils. They thoughtfully discuss the idea of how things change over time and realize that an unfamiliar object from the past has been replaced with a version that reflects today's technology or a new design. This conversation is the beginning of understanding history.

Everyday objects also offer an exciting opportunity for learning. In classrooms there is ample time for discovery and typically a more hands-on experience that is not frequently possible in galleries. Teachers ask open-ended questions and foster critical thinking throughout the process of learning.

Objects are also viewed in the context of other objects or as part of a collection. SEEC teachers and children create classroom collections that relate to projects or units of study. A collection of clay pots made by children might accompany a story of *The Empty Pot* by Demi or a display of baby shoes might connect to the idea of pairs. In a different unit of study, the collection of baby shoes might be part of children's personal timelines to indicate growth.

SEEC kindergartners are well acquainted with collections and the roles of individuals within museums. The children become curators of their own collections in the classroom, gathering artifacts, creating labels, making drawings, and arranging objects to tell a carefully crafted story. Not only does the child take on the role of curator and collections specialist, but she also serves as the docent or interpreter of the exhibit at its opening.

Executive Director Dr. Kimberlee Kiehl describes the SEEC experience as an opportunity for "children to be extraordinary, to wonder and to explore the world around them" (SEEC 2014).

At SEEC we believe that our job is to help children explore their questions, follow their interests, and develop their passions. We believe a classroom should not be a space within four walls but should include the community in which we live. We offer children days full of rich experiences that are presented in ways that are appropriate for their developmental level. We want children to leave SEEC excited about learning! (SEEC 2014)

Betsy Bowers, Deputy Director for the Center of Excellence at SEEC, offers a glimpse into a commonplace experience for children at SEEC. "When students use the Mammal Hall in Natural History, the art of Andy Warhol, and the Chinese scrolls at the Freer to make comparisons between different types of cats, the concept of critical thinking takes on a whole new meaning" (SEEC 2014).

> SEEC teachers use objects as tools to help children make tangible and personal connections to stories, museum pieces, and abstract concepts. Children use found objects to imitate a sculpture in the art museum, a tea set allows children to pretend to use an ancient Japanese set at the Freer Gallery of Art, and a kitchen strainer helps explain the eating habits of the beloved whale in the Natural History museum. Teachers use a mix of familiar objects from the child's home or classroom as well as special items from a teacher's collection. Children are encouraged to touch and examine each object during the lesson and later as objects are on display in the classroom throughout the unit of study. (Rachel Pucko, Master Teacher [2006-2012]; personal communication)

A museum-based approach to learning is not the same for all programs claiming a relationship to museum learning. And although a growing number of museum preschools are on the museum campus, others exist outside of the setting but have a close relationship with museums and museum-based pedagogy.

The Museum School, founded in 1949 as part of the Fort Worth Museum of Science and History, is recognized for its early innovation and seeks to advance learning for preschoolers through rich experiences with historical artifacts and science materials in the museum setting. The primary goal of the Museum School is to expand children's mental horizons "through vivid first-hand experiences about the wonderful and fascinating world of science." The school also encourages children to understand their world through a unique curriculum rich in "natural and physical sciences, history, and anthropology with art, music, and literature" (Fort Worth Museum of Science and History 2014). The Museum School continues to thrive today.

A more recent example of a museum-based approach for young children exists west of Boston in the newly defined partnership between the Lincoln Nursery School and DeCordova Sculpture Park and Museum. The partnership between the nursery school and the contemporary art museum began more than 60 years ago with informal class visits to DeCordova and led to a formalized partnership in 2010 and a move to the museum's campus. The program is heralded as "the first of its kind at a contemporary art museum in the United States" (DeCordova Museum and Sculpture Gardens, 2014) and offers a unique experience for preschoolers. The school is based on the belief "that children find meaning, build connections, and reveal their theories about the world through inquiry, play, materials, and relationships" (DeCordova Museum and Sculpture Gardens 2014). Inspired by a Reggio Emilia approach to learning, children explore the natural world, visit paintings and sculpture in galleries, meet with artists and other experts, and watch installations on the museum campus as they explore relevant concepts in their world. For children at Lincoln, the museum and sculpture gardens offer a natural connection to learning whether inside or outside of studio classrooms.

At the Rochester Museum & Science Center (RMSC) Preschool in New York, the museum is a special place for learning where children visit the galleries to make new discoveries around specific topics of interest. For example, children can explore many facets of bridge construction in a visit to a museum exhibit on building where children become architects, designers, and contractors.

Other museum preschools incorporate museum principles or methodologies into their practice by studying objects and creating collections to document learning. There are variations in programs claiming a museum-based approach to learning, yet all recognize fundamental principles that define museums. For each early childhood program, the vision reflects some essential aspect of the museum culture.

Early Childhood Criteria for Quality Practice

The National Association for the Education of Young Children

The National Association for the Education of Young Children (NAEYC) was established in 1964 to promote excellence in early childhood education and is known internationally for establishing best practice criteria. NAEYC updates its criteria to reflect current thinking about theory and practice, evolving to meet the needs of the ever-changing demographics that make up American society.

Prevailing thought about best practice places respect for the child at the highest level. Exemplary programs emphasize a child-centered approach in which learning is about the whole child—nurturing social, emotional, cognitive, and physical development—and where learning is individually paced to meet the unique nature and skills of each child. Educators evaluate the individual needs and establish positive teacher–child interactions, a highly valued feature of quality.

In addition to best practice criteria, NAEYC serves as an accrediting organization that offers early childhood programs a pathway for increasing program quality through self-study and validation. While every standard or benchmark identified by NAEYC may not fit museum programming, there is much to be learned from the research, publications, and experts leading the field in promoting high-quality early childhood education.

Classroom Assessment Scoring System

The Classroom Assessment Scoring System (CLASS) is a research-based tool for observing the quality of teacher-student interactions that defines desired elements of early childhood practice. This 2008 tool, based on developmental theory and research, offers common metrics for analyzing teachers' interactions with students regarding the quality of 1) emotional support in early childhood classrooms, such as positive climate, negative climate, teacher sensitivity, and regard for student perspectives; 2) classroom organization, including behavior management, productivity, and instructional learning formats; and 3) instructional support, including concept development, quality of feedback, and language modeling (Pianta et al. 2008).

One of the most critical elements of CLASS is concept development. Pianta et al. (2008) identify desired teacher behaviors that foster analysis and reasoning, creativity, integration of new ideas, and connections to the real world. The authors purport that interactions between teachers and children are paramount in shaping learning outcomes. CLASS is gaining prominence as the leading assessment tool for early childhood learning and is widely used by Head Start and other programs.

CLASS also has merit for museum practitioners because it identifies the most important variables for understanding how adult–student interactions affect desired outcomes for cognitive development and defines strategies to promote higher-order thinking and creativity. These goals are not only relevant for young children in formal and informal learning environments, but have application for families and other groups in museums as well.

Conclusion

Early learning has been a topic of research and interest for decades, particularly in the broader context of families and schools. Traditional museums have more recently joined the early learning movement and are now establishing programs and exhibits for this audience. By crossing boundaries between formal and informal learning, museum professionals can build on established research and experience.

Early childhood models valued today and the practices respected by experts in the field offer museum educators a framework for developing museum programs and spaces for little ones. What are those lessons or principles that deserve attention from the museum community?

- Demonstrate genuine respect for each and every child
- Design programs that are child-centered
- Value children's ideas and perspectives
- Make learning relevant and meaningful
- Build on children's interests and areas of common knowledge
- Create experiences that engage children through their senses
- Plan opportunities that allow exploration and discovery
- Incorporate inquiry within programming
- Anticipate and embrace opportunities for play and social interaction

Museum professionals need to think deeply about each of the principles representing good practice in early childhood learning and decide how these ideas translate to new settings with unique characteristics. With some careful culling, there are gems hidden within the early childhood models that align perfectly with a particular museum's mission and goals. Above all else, approaching the development of museum programs for early learning with eyes open to the research and practice established in the early childhood field can at the very least be an excellent starting point for museum practitioners.

Chapter Five

Best Practice: Key Concepts

"Knowing is a process, not a product."

—*Jerome Bruner*

Introduction

In education, the term *best practice* is often bandied about in connection with an approach to learning that offers guidelines for teaching and reflects a certain set of values or beliefs that define what that looks like. In actuality, best practice is not fixed, but rather shaped by a variety of factors that reflect social and cultural contexts as well as desired outcomes.

Best practices, while varied, can be situated within a theoretical framework that defines our thinking about teaching and learning. Jerome Bruner's profound belief in learning as a process offers that framework, which shapes our thinking about educational practice today.

> To instruct someone . . . is not a matter of getting him to commit results to mind. Rather, it is to teach him to participate in the process that makes possible the establishment of knowledge. We teach a subject not to produce little living libraries on that subject, but rather to get a student to think mathematically for himself, to consider matters as an historian does, to take part in the process of knowledge-getting. Knowing is a process not a product. (Bruner 1966, p. 72)

Rather than a defined methodology, educational practice should be a dynamic process set within a distinct framework of beliefs that evolve and mirror new perspectives. Best practice changes to reflect new insights gleaned from experience and an understanding of the ever-changing nature of society and the needs of learners. As the world changes, context for learning changes as well and with it our need to reflect on our practice and revise our thinking to meet the new norm.

Current thinking about best practice for early learning can be considered in the context of ideas proven to be effective across a wide variety of settings and with varied groups of children rather than as the final word on practice. The goal is to learn from research and experience, and then make revisions that align with new knowledge. This process leads to better service for young visitors.

Engaging Young Children in Museums, by Sharon E. Shaffer, 88–100. © 2015 Left Coast Press, Inc. All rights reserved.

Thinking about effective practice requires a perspective that goes beyond the methodology of engaging children in learning by addressing the culture of the institution in which the learning takes place. By defining parameters of organizational culture that support and enhance early learning initiatives, we further define criteria to describe effective practice.

Broad-based ideas culled from experience in the field offer a beginning point for practitioners in museums. Programs designed with these key concepts in mind are apt to be more effective for an audience of young children and their companions.

- Build consensus around early learning in the museum through collaboration across departments.
- Create a welcoming environment that offers emotional and physical comfort essential for young children and their families.
- Build capacity of educators and facilitators to ensure an understanding of the audience (children and families), modeling desired learning theory in training.
- Align strategies and techniques with the characteristics of children as learners to make the experience one that will engage little ones, nurture their curiosity, and encourage meaningful connections.
- Recognize that early learning is a concept that is dynamic and requires an open mind to new ideas and future discoveries about learning.

By keeping each of these factors in mind, the process of planning for young children begins.

Build Consensus for Early Learning in the Museum

Until recently, museums have focused attention on audiences other than young children; for many institutions, even for those who welcome little ones to their galleries, this is uncharted territory in which the ideas and the audience are relatively new to many practitioners. As with any change, there will be declarations of support as well as expressions of concern, and this is certainly true for early learning in museums.

There are a many reasons to invest in early learning. It may be linked primarily to a desire or need to build audience participation or in response to community interest in programming for young children, which in turn leads to expanding programs or other opportunities to meet a need. It is not uncommon for museums to respond to the great demand expressed by parents, preschools in the community, city officials, and others interested in early learning.

In some cases, the decision to invest in early learning is rooted in politics and resource opportunities in which funding for this audience brings new resources to an institution at a time of declining revenue. One museum candidly acknowledged pursuing funding for early learning specifically for its availability rather than for the museum's interest in serving this audience. With challenging economic times and cuts in funding sources, museums are inclined to look for opportunities that are more readily available. In some cases, the pursuit of funds specified for early learning introduces more than a new revenue source; it broadens the audience served and expands the reach of the museum within the community. And while the initial impetus for seeking funding may be economic in nature, there are other benefits: the museum's image will likely be enhanced by the expansion of programs beneficial to the community, and at the same time the museum establishes relationships with families, building patrons for the future. This is a win-win situation for the museum and the community.

There are other drivers of early learning in today's world, often related to social beliefs or values. Investing in the education of young children is a reflection of the times. By the turn of the twenty-first century the early learning field had gained popularity and was perceived as a priority across the nation unparalleled in previous times. Interest in early learning grew not only in the United States, but also around the world. Even family-friendly museums of 2000 focused on children aged six and older as part of families, but as it became clear that younger children were also frequent visitors, museums redefined the audience to include three- to six-year-olds as a primary audience within families.

For many of these reasons, the museum community's awareness and value of early learning has grown, and with it a new perspective on opportunities for engaging young children in experiences with art, artifacts, and objects from the natural world. Museums developed public programs for preschoolers from the school sector and the family sector; established museum-based schools outside of the museum offered models for study by educators in the field. With increasing social acceptance, the movement to serve younger children was no longer a dream of a few, but an ambition for many.

When embarking on a new initiative, it is important to share the rationale underlying the decision. It is a time to engage colleagues in open discussion and experimentation about programming for young children to seek a common understanding of possibilities. Some experimental programs will succeed; others will fail. But the collaborative effort to identify opportunities and reflect on outcomes is an essential part of the process.

This might also be an appropriate time to clearly articulate benefits anticipated for visitors and for the organization by sharing current research and theory that supports the effort. And although the research is scant, it is growing along with reports funded by organizations like the Pew Charitable Trust and the Institute of Museum and Library Services (IMLS). A recent literature review commissioned by the Smithsonian Early Enrichment

Center (SEEC) engaged Mary Ellen Munley (MEM & Associates) to identify and summarize research findings related to young children in museums. In the review, Munley highlighted "the qualities of museums that foster learning in young children—real artifacts, immersive exhibits, and familiar contexts" (Denver Art Museum 2013, p.4). The conversation about early learning is enhanced by academic research and reports from the field.

Under the best of circumstances, an early childhood initiative is backed or initiated by a group of like-minded museum professionals who recognize the potential of early learning and see opportunities for this audience. By sharing this passion with colleagues, members of the cohort can hopefully increase support across the institution. This was the case in the mid-1980s at the Philadelphia Museum of Art when developing *Museum Looks and Picture Books*, an innovative, gallery-based preschool program (Philadelphia Museum of Art 2014). Advocacy came from within the education department, but gained greater acceptance across the museum with support from museum leadership. In this way, programming for young children took root; today, the community recognizes it as an important program and contribution to area schools and families.

At times, the idea comes from the vision of one individual, shared with others, quietly at first but with passion and intentionality that develops over time as colleagues are carefully introduced to the ideas and brought on board. According to Heather Nielsen, Associate Director of Education and Master Teacher for Native Arts and New World at the Denver Art Museum (DAM), this describes the leadership of Patterson Williams (Director of Education from 1979 to 2002; Co-Director of Education from 2002 to 2004), and her role as an advocate for serving young visitors. This effort came at a time when the museum defined itself as a place primarily for adult audiences, even though there were many other visitors in the galleries. Williams' deep commitment to welcoming young children and their families in the early days of her tenure laid the groundwork for what was to become a hallmark of DAM in future years.

DAM continued to invest in young visitors, but with greater interest and buy-in across the organization. In 1998, a core team of educators dedicated to family learning "called on the entire education department and many other museum departments such as marketing and security" to join the effort to ensure institution-wide support and messaging to the public (Denver Art Museum 2002, p. 6). The core team viewed establishing DAM as a family destination a museum-wide effort.

There are also organizations that see the value of early learning in relationship to the mission and develop educational programs with this audience in mind. The Smithsonian National Museum of African American History and Culture (NMAAHC), even in the planning phase, has already acknowledged the importance of bringing young children into the fold, a belief represented at all levels of the institution from Founding Director Lonnie Bunch to educators and curators. As a museum defined by a commitment to "stimulate dialogue about race" (NMAAHC 2014), it is developing a center that caters to young visitors to engage them in conversation about perceptions of race and concepts of fairness. Knowing that identity is shaped early in life, experts in the museum believe that conversations about race are apt to have greater impact if introduced at an early age.

In some settings, the dedication and passion displayed for early learning is met with skepticism. The idea of young children in traditional galleries, particularly in history and art museums, is and has been perceived at times in a less than positive light, with worries about the safety of the artifacts or works of art as well as uncertainty about the possible benefits that could come from such an experience. There are some who simply believe that young children are not within the mission of the museum. Those with this perspective regard very young children as unsophisticated in their ability to learn or engage in any meaningful way with artifacts, paintings, or sculpture because of a seemingly limited cognitive capacity, but research and experience disproves this point of view. Fortunately, that perspective is less pervasive as the field demonstrates greater acceptance of young museumgoers.

To sway skeptics, supporters within the museum community have demonstrated tireless effort and resilience over the years to convince less-than-receptive colleagues. They have approached this task by presenting research from the field, by collecting information about need through community surveys, and by examining pilot programs that have demonstrated success, building a case for serving young children. Over time, acceptance for early learning has grown and values have shifted, leading to an increase in related programs in traditional museums.

The Denver Art Museum (DAM) is a model of child-friendly and family-friendly museumgoing, a culture that developed over its long history. As early as the 1950s, the museum included a center for children's art activities, an early indicator of the institution's commitment to young museumgoers and their families that would later define the organization. By 2000, the art museum was firmly focused on family learning, and by 2013 revised its target audience within families to reflect a broader spectrum of ages, acknowledging "the biggest catalyst for growth of DAM family programs" as "children between the ages of 3 and 5" (Denver Art Museum 2013, p. 4).

This bold tradition of embracing the young child as a prominent member of the museum community is evident in the family-friendly approach that "is fully integrated into the galleries through a unique partnership between curators, designers, and educators for each discipline" (Denver Art Museum 2014). Experimental activities such as the development of gallery backpacks laid the groundwork for more permanent family-friendly installations (Figure 5.1).

Figure 5.1. Families at the Denver Art Museum explore the American Indian galleries through games, puzzles, and artmaking activities from the "Horses on Parade" backpack designed for three- to five-year-olds. Photo courtesy of the Denver Art Museum.

Today, children and their companions navigate galleries with direction from the fun-loving mascot Seymour, a friendly monkey based on a pre-Columbian ceramic vessel in the permanent collection. While in the galleries, families enjoy the social experience of exploring uniquely designed activities for art making, games, and puzzles. And beyond the galleries, families visit the *Just For Fun Center* to explore, build, and imagine, or spend time in the *Kids Corner* for opportunities to make connections to the visual world of paintings and sculpture that are seemingly endless. Those with toddlers join Create Playdate and Totspot Sunday for programs created for the young, novice museum visitor. Each experience is memorable and leaves family members young and old excited about the possibility of returning to the art museum.

For this institution as for many others, consensus on early learning grew over time through advocacy of individuals within the institution. Today, DAM is recognized as a family-friendly place where one of its most important assets is how it values all members of the community.

Finding consensus through collaboration across departments and levels of hierarchy within the museum increases the likelihood of long-term success. Current research, models of practice, and anecdotal evidence of positive impact can make a difference in how young children are viewed and the future of programs for this audience.

Create a Welcoming Environment for Children

It takes just one step inside a museum for visitors to know whether they belong. Messages are embedded in the visual environment and in the social interactions of staff. This is true not only for children, but for all audiences. What is the first impression for the visitor? How can museums create a welcoming environment that speaks to families and children?

Museums take great pride in their thoughtful approach to shaping the visual environment. This same care can make a difference in the message that is conveyed when visitors enter the museum. And while the physical environment needs to invite and welcome visitors, including our youngest museumgoers, the attitudes and actions of the staff are even more important. How do museums greet young visitors? What messages are conveyed to parents and children when they arrive at the museum? Is it clear that there are special experiences for young children, or that the museum offers experiences that will engage and delight little ones? When the museum is confident that a rewarding experience awaits children and their partners, the feeling comes across to visitors and establishes a positive starting point.

Personal connections between museum staff and children set the tone for a visit. A simple smile or friendly hello establishes a feeling of welcome. It only takes a few innocent remarks or an unfriendly expression that suggests the visitor has entered the museum in error to make everyone ill at ease. This is less likely to happen when there is consensus and support across the organization, and when everyone in the museum recognizes the positive experiences that can be offered to young visitors.

A welcoming environment is now more the norm than at any other time in the past. It is likely that children and families are greeted with a warm smile by most. In fact, there are museums that present young visitors with stickers, a special guide, or an invitation to take part in events designed for the young. The ideal is, of course, that everyone is on board with this important first step in creating positive experiences for young visitors and their families as well as for preschoolers visiting museums with their classes.

Another important component of this welcoming environment relates to creating a sense of comfort. This may sound trite to some, but families and teachers acknowledge this as critical to a successful visit to a museum. Comfort can be physical—appropriate places to sit, eat, change diapers—as well as a sense of familiarity in experiences within the museum. Familiar activities that children love and enjoy in their lives, such as reading stories, play, social interaction, and freedom of choice, increase the sense of comfort when woven artfully into museum experiences. By creating a culture that respects the needs of the child and his family, the museum demonstrates its interest and support for this audience of young museumgoers.

Build Capacity of Educators and Interpreters

Many museum educators have some formal coursework in educational theory and practice, but until recently, few had a strong understanding of young children and how they learn. It is the rare museum that has an early childhood specialist on staff, although this is changing as well with the growing interest in early learning. The Smithsonian's National Air and Space Museum is one of those rare places where an entire department is dedicated to early learning and is further blessed with the support of an endowment designated specifically to support early childhood education in the museum.

It is not uncommon for museums to hire content specialists—art historians, science experts, or history enthusiasts—for their education departments rather than trained educators. And while these individuals bring incredible strength in content knowledge, there is a need to build capacity for understanding how people learn and develop knowledge of effective teaching strategies that will engage audiences, particularly the audience of young children and their families. Knowledge of young children, when complemented by an understanding of family learning, establishes a baseline for design of effective programs and exhibitions.

This challenge is often evident in small or rural museums where staff members are expected to wear many hats. And while nearly impossible to be an expert in multiple areas, museum expertise more often than not aligns with the collection rather than with educational theory and practice.

Volunteers, or docents, are critical to many education departments and play an important role in gallery tours and student programs. Though these individuals are typically passionate about museums and collections, their background varies greatly and is one factor that can make a difference in the quality of visitor experiences. Therefore, training is a vital component of preparing volunteers for the role of leading programs for the public. One effective technique is to model desired practices for early learning in galleries.

It is often said that we teach the way that we were taught. This presents us with a dilemma for moving beyond old notions of learning and bringing new perspectives to visitor experience. If we subscribe to the new ideas represented in current learning theory, we need to model and engage our educators and gallery interpreters in this new way of thinking.

It makes sense for training to be consistent with the values, beliefs, and expectations for programming. For individuals who believe that learning is an active process and that people construct knowledge through personal interaction with their environment, designing training that encourages active participation is optimal. Lecturing to a group of educators about the benefits of active learning doesn't make much sense. Modeling also gives facilitators an example of what the museum experience might look like. By modeling inquiry-based learning during training, it is easier for an educator or docent to replicate the strategy in future gallery programs.

More and more museums are investing in professional development to educate staff members and volunteers to ensure high-quality programs. The National Gallery of Art (NGA) in Washington, DC, is an excellent model for building staff capacity through internal and external training opportunities. Ongoing professional development, a hallmark of NGA, is considered a worthy investment, particularly for the volunteer corps who leads school tours. According to Heidi Hinish, Head of the Department of Teacher, School, and Family Programs at NGA, specialized sessions led by experts in the field introduce volunteers to "the characteristics of young children, educational theories that speak to the range of children's developmental levels, and strategies for effectively teaching young children in the art museum. Specialists in drama, theater, and movement techniques have also led docent workshops, informing our work with young children and encouraging our docents to experiment with more playful approaches to teaching" (H. Hinish, personal communication, 2014).

Hinish also said "docent education programs are strongly influenced by Ron Ritchhart's *Cultures of Thinking* from Harvard's Project Zero research and framework" (H. Hinish, personal communication, 2014). In training sessions, docents develop an understanding of Project Zero's thinking routines, "easy to use mini-strategies" (Visible Thinking 2014), and then apply techniques as they lead school tours. NGA places great value on building the capacities of their educators and interpreters.

The Denver Art Museum is similarly committed to supporting the professional development and growth of staff members. This is captured in their 2013 report, *Kids and Their Grownups*, which identifies professional development as an important goal for the institution. The museum invests in building "a core group of staff members who are individually and collectively engaged in evaluations and reflective practice" (Denver Art Museum 2013, p. 2). One noteworthy area identified was evaluation and the emphasis on staff listening directly to families. To support educators in learning about evaluation, "consultants Daryl Fischer and Kathleen Tinworth wove capacity building through the project from start to finish, involving staff members in identifying research questions and collecting data" (Denver Art Museum, 2013, p. 23).

This process of building capacity can take many shapes, as evidenced by these examples. The goal is to develop essential skills for working with young children and their families, whether in facility design, program development, or evaluation.

Align Strategies and Techniques with Learning Theory

In creating exhibition space or developing early learning programs, the key is understanding young children and how they learn as individuals and in the social context of families, and then crafting strategies that align with that knowledge. Most people have some experience with children, from family ties to neighborhood encounters, and can describe the characteristics associated with preschoolers and kindergartners based on informal observations.

To anyone who spends time with preschoolers, it is apparent that children are primarily active learners and that their senses play a critical role in how they construct meaning about their world. With this perspective in mind, it would then be logical to consider crafting museum programs that are active and engage the senses, rather than designing programs that are primarily teacher-centered such as information tours. Examining distinct characteristics that define the learning style leads to more effective planning for young visitors.

Professional training that encourages museum professionals to reflect on personal beliefs about children and how they learn is a good starting point for demystifying early learning in museums. Educators and interpreters gain confidence with increased knowledge of cognitive development that comes from an introduction to educational theory relevant to early learning. It isn't essential to become an expert, but it is important to grasp key ideas that provide insight into the learning process of the young.

Museums are more likely to meet the educational needs of preschoolers and kindergartners when there is a strong correlation between the learning style of young children and the strategies integrated into gallery programs. As museums expand background knowledge of educators and interpreters, practices become more engaging and meaningful.

Figure 5.2. Sculptures by David Smith at the National Gallery of Art: Circle I, 1962; Circle II, 1962; Circle III, 1962. © The Estate of David Smith/ Licensed by VAGA, New York, NY.

Docents at the National Gallery of Art look at sculpture in the gallery through the eyes of a child. They view painted steel sculptures by David Smith (1962): *Circle I, Circle II,* and *Circle III* (Figure 5.2). There are distinctive shapes—circles, semi-circles, and long, narrow rectangles—that the artist incorporated into large compositions. An inquiry-based discussion grounds the experience as docents are encouraged to look, reflect, analyze, and connect with the art from a personal point of view, thinking about observations that children might make. Language is but one aspect of the exploration.

Central to the experience is active learning. Docents are presented with cut-out shapes similar to those used by the artist and are then invited to work collaboratively to create compositions on the marble floor inspired by Smith's art. As the activity progresses, provocative questions challenge the participants. *How did you decide which shapes to place next to one another? How could you move the shapes to create a new sculpture? How are our sculptures similar to David Smith's works of art? How are they different? If you could add something new to one of the sculptures, what would it be?* By modeling inquiry-based exploration, active learning, and collaboration, the training actively engages docents. They are learning through experience, which fits into the constructivist model. This approach also spurs conversation not only about what strategies were integrated into the lesson, but why these strategies fit with the learning style of young children.

Recognize Early Learning as a Dynamic Concept that Requires an Open Mind toward New Ideas

In the past 25 years there have been significant changes in society, cultural norms, museum practices, demographics, and scientific discoveries. Clearly change is not compartmentalized within one specific area, but has implications across many aspects of society.

Museums exist within a global society, which requires that educators think about the world in a new and different way. This global access offers opportunities to learn from colleagues around the world and engage in dialogue about issues and practices pertinent to almost any topic of interest. For museum professionals, the world's stage offers insight into educational theories and practices that reflect thinking beyond our local or national community.

Educators also are well aware of changing demographics within our communities and across our nation, which has noteworthy implications for museums and the people they serve. Museum professionals are thinking about visitors with the understanding that personal experience contributes to the interpretation of exhibitions. As social norms evolve, the museum practitioner's ideas and interactions with visitors must reflect the new norms as well.

A museum experience 25 years ago may not be relevant for audiences visiting museums today. As minorities of the past become the majority culture of the future, museums are interested in making the museum a place for all people, not simply serving those who fit past models. This is equally important for practitioners thinking about young audiences. Programs that make connections between the cultural background and experiences of diverse young visitors are likely to resonate and encourage a stronger connection to the museum.

In looking back over the past 25 years, one of the most striking differences is the technological advances that have changed America's culture and the way people interact with one another. In the 1980s or early 1990s, it would have been difficult to imagine the world of today with easy global access through the Internet, instant communication with people around the world, and a perception of social engagement that takes place in a virtual world rather than in a favorite restaurant. And this just touches the surface of technology in today's world.

In museums, teens and tweens, and probably young adults, share their experiences through photographs that are instantly uploaded to Instagram and Facebook. They weigh in with their thoughts on Twitter and post favorite images on Pinterest. Understanding technology and the possibilities for connecting children to artifacts and works of art or engaging families in the museum is a topic for careful consideration by professionals in the museum field.

Most important is keeping an open mind, realizing that opportunities are vastly different in today's global world. It may not be possible to predict or anticipate what changes the future will bring, but what is certain is that change is inevitable and that museum professionals must be prepared to consider the relevance and impact on exhibition design and programming for children and families.

Conclusion

Best practice describes more than an educational theory about learning, but suggests a culture that supports and nurtures learning based on a set of shared beliefs. While Jerome Bruner's belief that "knowledge is a process, not a product" (1966, p. 72) is a statement about learning, it also has meaning in a broader sense. Experts believe that best practice is not a stagnant set of practices describing what to do, but a dynamic assimilation of factors that engage and inform actions as educators and practitioners.

Most of all, best practice defines a culture surrounding the museum professional's work, embedded in an environment that is physical and social in nature. Knowledge of educational theory and the work of cognitive theorists such as Piaget and Vygotsky, as described in chapter 3 of this book, is critical to that understanding. A museum's commitment to early learning is evident in the personal interactions of staff as they open the doors to welcome children, literally and figuratively, as well as in the respect for children in the design of physical space and programs. Understanding young children and families in the context of museum learning is essential for serving this important constituency.

Delving more deeply into the task of building capacity within the museum—the knowledge and skills of individuals who are the lifeline of museum experiences—is the subject of the next chapter. This is certainly the foundation for early childhood programming in museums. It is not always possible to hire specialists who possess expertise in early childhood education as well as in museum learning, but it is possible to provide training to increase knowledge and skills that lead to more effective leadership, programming, and engagement of young audiences and their companions. In the next chapter, I explore practical ideas to engage educators, docents, and facilitators in thinking about the characteristics of young children and families as learners as well as examine proven strategies for reaching this audience in galleries.

Chapter Six

Best Practice: A Foundation for Early Childhood Programming in Museums

> "Learning and teaching should not stand on opposite banks and just watch the river flow by; instead, they should embark together on a journey down the water. Through an active, reciprocal exchange, teaching can strengthen learning how to learn."
>
> —*Loris Malaguzzi*

Introduction

As museums ponder early learning initiatives, there is a need to focus attention on gallery staff: educators, volunteer interpreters, facilitators, and in fact all museum staff serving the public.

- What is the knowledge base related to cognition and developmental theory of individuals working closely with young audiences and their companions?
- How are museums building capacity of educators and interpreters who affect the quality of the child's experience or a family's experience?
- Are practices aligned with current theory?
- Are individuals facilitating programs engaged in continuous reflection and exposure to new ideas to improve practice?

The educator or facilitator is at the heart of high-quality museum programming. To ensure quality, museums have a responsibility to invest in the educators tasked with developing and engaging young children and their families. For most museums, that responsibility extends beyond the museum educators carefully hired by the institution to include volunteer interpreters or educators, often referred to as *docents*. It is time well spent to carefully select and train individuals who will be responsible for guiding and shaping experiences for young children and their companions.

This investment creates a culture that values learning and builds capacity of individuals responsible for the design and implementation of high-quality

Engaging Young Children in Museums, by Sharon E. Shaffer, 101–130. © 2015 Left Coast Press, Inc.

programs. It also encourages a community of learning that consists of personal reflection and open-minded contemplation of relevant theory and practice. By its very nature, a well-trained cadre of educators strengthens the quality of programming within the museum.

The Heart of Education at the Museum: Educators, Facilitators, and Volunteers

The quality of education within the museum is closely tied to the knowledge, expertise, and attitude of the educators and volunteer corps responsible for programming. For that reason, organizations offer professional development opportunities to strengthen background knowledge in theory and practice, prepare the workforce for their role in galleries, and infuse an approach to learning that reflects the ideological perspective of the institution.

Training programs for educators and facilitators, who frequently are volunteers, are as diverse as the museums they serve. At times, museums will hire an expert from the field as a consultant to introduce pedagogical practices or instill new perspectives into the culture of the organization. And although museum educators are sometimes in the role of learner, they more frequently are tasked with designing and leading training for interpreters.

In many cases, the volunteers/docents joining forces with the museum come from a wide range of backgrounds. While some arrive at the museum with formal studies in education and experience in classrooms, few are experts in early learning. Within the volunteer corps there are content experts with extensive knowledge of history, science, art, or culture that reflects the mission of the museum. Others are simply interested in the museum and its collection with a desire to share their passion and talents for the good of the community.

The responsibilities of docents vary from serving as tour guides or lecturers to greeting visitors entering the museum. The settings for engaging visitors differ as well from galleries to classrooms, with interactions ranging from dialogue about objects showcased on education carts to structured programs or highlight tours. Above all else, dedicated volunteers strive to unlock the mysteries of museum collections and connect visitors to the wonder of history, science, art, and culture through the stories embedded in cultural artifacts, scientific specimens, and works of art. In science centers and children's museums, volunteers play an important role as they support young visitors and families in exploring concepts through hands-on experiences.

Many museums depend upon the generosity of volunteers. By providing a well-conceived plan for professional development, the museum acknowledges the value of docents and establishes a culture committed to lifelong learning as a model. A formal course of study validates the work as important and establishes credibility for those engaged in the educational endeavors of the museum. By all accounts, it is well worth the investment.

Professional Development for Gallery Staff

Most museum educators value professional development and see it as essential for creating a strong cadre of gallery facilitators. The approach and depth of training may differ, but the practice is prevalent throughout the field. While many museums privilege content over methodology, the best training programs are comprehensive and include both. When educators possess knowledge of the collection, they are more likely to engage visitors in meaningful dialogue and share accurate information that enriches the gallery experience. For everyone engaging with visitors, it is equally important to understand the methodology that underlies the learning process.

What does this intersection of content and methodology look like for young visitors? A balance is present at the art museum when preschoolers learn about Josef Albers' interest and exploration of color by listening to *An Eye for Color: The Story of Josef Albers* (Wing 2009) and then creating their own color experiments with paper squares of various sizes and colors in the gallery. This experience encourages preschoolers to look at art in the gallery, respond to what they see, learn about the artist and his ideas, make personal connections by becoming friends with the artist through the story, and then actively test new ideas about color interaction in front of a masterpiece by Albers. Exploring color can be a process of collaborative experimentation between a child and adult or a child and her peers. The merging of content with methodology creates an experience of quality that honors the content related to the artist while also respecting the learning style of the young visitor.

When methodology and learning theory hold equal rank with content, educators and docents develop a deep understanding of the process of learning and techniques for engaging audiences with the content of the collection.

In today's world, where museums value visitor engagement and dialogue in the gallery, it is important to recognize that this is a shift from past beliefs in which a guided tour with lecture represented the norm. With this change in paradigm it is important to consider whether educators and docents are adequately prepared with the necessary skills to ask probing questions or encourage visitors to construct meaning about the objects on display. This seems so simplistic, and yet when docents or facilitators are in transition between the old and the new, becoming comfortable with open-ended questions that require an interchange of ideas is not always natural and entails thought and practice.

Training sessions that introduce a structured approach to questioning will build skill and confidence for docents and educators. Thinking Routines, an artfully crafted approach developed by Harvard's Project Zero, is one example that offers a variety of strategies. "See, Think, Wonder" is a well-known Thinking Routine based on three simple questions: *What do you see? What do you think? What do you wonder?* (Visible Thinking, 2014). The open-ended approach encourages visitors to observe, interpret, and extend their thinking about an object or work of art and can be applied to a wide variety of audience experiences. Educators and docents will gain practical skills for engaging visitors as well as confidence in their abilities when strategies are introduced and practiced during training sessions.

When training reflects today's thinking about gallery practice and acknowledges the diversity of visitors and their unique styles of learning, museums build educator capacity and increase the quality of educational experiences afforded to all. Building this foundation reaps benefits for the visitor and the museum.

There are many valuable resources available to guide leaders in planning professional development for staff. *The Museum Educator's Manual* (Johnson et al. 2009) features guidelines for working with volunteers and suggests a range of topics to consider when designing training for docents. *The Docent Handbook* by the National Docent Symposium Council (2001) offers an approach to training with topics that range from audience and visitor learning styles to sensitive issues and strategies for engaging the public.

The key to the training process is linking decision-making about methodologies and content to include in training to the goals and philosophical beliefs of the organization as well as understanding baseline knowledge of docents and other facilitators. A successful plan for professional development will incorporate meaningful experiences that engage participants in building personal knowledge and skills to support a variety of audiences.

Planning the Training

Planning professional development sessions takes time and thought. Some sessions will be dedicated to content related to the museum (the *what*), while other sessions will introduce educational theories and strategies for engaging young audiences (the *why and how*). This chapter addresses the latter, leaving the content to educators and curators.

Modeling a constructivist approach, accompanied by an explanation, sets the tone for training and encourages participants to think about this experience as conversation rather than a presentation. Participants gain insight and understanding about object-based methodologies when they are personally engaged in the process of learning. They recognize that social interaction and exploration of tangible objects add a dimension to learning that is missing when concepts are presented only through words.

Training that models active learning trumps a simple lecture and demonstrates more clearly what object-based learning looks like and why it is important. When training encourages independent discovery or collaborative learning, educators and interpreters become active participants in the process, gaining new insight that will ultimately lead to more effective teaching strategies for actively engaging audiences in museums.

Educators, docents, and facilitators, as individuals and as a group, have different needs, as does the education department. Individuals learn in many different ways. The sequence of activities presented in this chapter may suit some groups but not others, but offers a starting point for engaging individuals who interface with the public. Professional development designed around the needs of the group and incorporating a variety of resources is likely to be most helpful in building capacity of the cohort. The experiences described here provide ideas for planning, but it is still important to keep in mind the unique nature of the group in training.

Introductory Activity for Educator Training

Module I: Museum Goals: A Conversation

Set the stage for training with a few simple, yet provocative questions that encourage participants to think about goals for young museum visitors.

- Is the museum experience about learning or rather about a fun-filled afternoon with family members?
- Is the visit intended to broaden horizons or allow a child to explore a personal interest?
- What are the opportunities for learning in the museum?
- How might a child be influenced by the experience?
- How are the museum's goals different from those of the visitor?

In *Learning from Museums: Visitor Experiences and the Making of Meaning,* John Falk and Lynn Dierking (2000) indicate that visitors articulate many different reasons for visiting museums, but that learning is often at the core of the intended experience. The rationale for museum visits is complex and worth spending some time considering.

For museum educators, it is important to understand the audience of young children and families, and their goals for visiting the museum. The initial training session offers a perfect opportunity for those interfacing with this audience to think about possible goals by answering a simple question: In an ideal world, what outcomes do we want for our young visitors?

The question might shift slightly if the training is focused more on family engagement: In an ideal world, what outcomes do we want for our young visitors and their adult partners? Ask participants to work in small groups to discuss the module question(s) in Appendix A, listing desired outcomes from museum visits. Be clear that there are many possibilities rather than one right point of view. After the discussion, typically about 10 to 15 minutes, have each group share major points and describe the value of each idea.

The value of this exercise relies upon trusting participants to thoughtfully identify ideas about purpose without any artificial parameters. The cohort needs to become personally invested in this discussion. Although there is a range of ideas that typically arise during small group discussions, the ideas generated by the group are most important. Ideas listed here are best added only after participants share their comments.

As training sessions continue, return to the Museum Goals identified by the group during the Module I discussion as a reminder of desired outcomes. Think about specific programs and activities to decide how they align with desired goals.

Typical Museum Goals as Defined by Educators

- Broaden children's horizons and introduce the mysteries of the world
- Offer opportunities for exposure to content and concepts related to the mission of the museum and its exhibitions
- Strengthen the perception of a museum as a place where children belong
- Introduce children to the idea that a museum is a place to learn
- Encourage collaborative learning and shared meaning making
- Build a relationship between children/families and the museum
- Develop future patrons
- Engage, excite, and inspire: and offer a place to have fun!

Understanding Audience

Module II: Characteristics Of Young Children: Defining the Learning Style

With a sense of purpose defined for early learning programming, it is now time to think more deeply about the audience of young children. For anyone who has spent time with anyone younger than age five, it is apparent that little ones possess a natural curiosity and desire to learn. They have a zest for exploring their world and make meaning through their encounters with the environment. They learn through social interactions. In many cases, it is clear that there is an internal thought process that accompanies action, even though the ideas are not verbally expressed. Based upon experience and informal observations from the past, participants will have relevant memories to define characteristics of young children and then consider how these attributes contribute to learning. Some educators will be able to draw upon knowledge of cognitive developmental theory, and can share ideas about how theories align with observations shared by the group.

This discussion naturally follows the conversation about the purpose or goals for museum experiences. Ask participants to close their eyes and imagine a young child. What is she doing? How is she expressing her curiosity? What words would you use to describe the behaviors of young children? What distinguishes the learning style of young children from others? The central question is: What do we know about young children and how they learn?

Responses are far-ranging and typically include sentiments similar to these: *Children are busy and active. They explore their environment using their senses. Children learn through play. They use their imagination as part of play. Children express curiosity and ask lots of questions. Each child is unique. Children have personal interests that influence how they spend their time. Children interact socially and often mimic the behavior of others.*

Participants in training can work in small groups using the prompts in Appendix B and then report findings, or this can be a large group discussion. Record the personal observations on chart paper for later reference and think about possible connections to specific educational theorists supporting the ideas noted. This conversation is comfortable for most people since everyone has some experience with children, however informal, and from that experience come personal impressions. Observations will take on new meaning as they are later connected to theories of learning. Review the list of characteristics with the group. Return to the ideas in later sessions when determining appropriate strategies for early learning initiatives. Effective programs align teaching strategies with characteristics of learning.

It is sometimes helpful to organize ideas into broader statements that capture the main ideas about early learning. Group the observations offered in training based on common characteristics to create a Statement of Beliefs that describe children and how they learn.

Statement of Beliefs about How Children Learn

- We know that children are **active** participants in the learning process.
- We understand that children explore their environment and make meaning about their world through their **senses**.
- We recognize that children look for similarities and differences, and **sort, order,** and **classify** ideas/objects by common attributes, grouping by themes.
- We know that young children learn through **play** and recreate their understanding of the world and how it works through imaginative scenarios.
- We know that children are **social beings** and learn from interactions with others by observing, modeling, and imitating.
- We know that children are **inquisitive** and ask questions to make sense about what they see happening in their world.
- We know that children see their world as a narrative and gain meaning about their own experiences and those of others through **storytelling**.
- We believe children learn best through **authentic experiences** and that objects are tangible and concrete entry points for understanding the abstract world.

In addition to the discussion of young children as learners, individuals working with this audience will also benefit from looking closely at family groups. Family audiences have been part of museums for some time, but it wasn't until the mid- to late 1970s that researchers focused on family learning (Falk and Dierking 2013). In the 1980s, the research "identified families as a major audience and unique learning group of mixed ages and backgrounds" (Falk and Dierking 2013, p. 150), a topic still important in museums today.

Family Learning

Take some time to discuss family learning. How is family learning different from an experience dedicated exclusively to young children? Research suggests "families attempt to find shared meaning in exhibitions" (Falk and Dierking 2013, p. 151). Questions that provide thoughtful discussions will encourage educators to explore the concept of family learning or family engagement.

- What does family learning look like?
- How do families spend their time in museums?
- How do adults define the purpose of the museum experience and how does this mesh with the ideas of young visitors?
- What role might facilitators play in helping families create shared meaning from exhibitions?
- What issues arise and what strategies work best to address those concerns?

In addition to the attributes typically associated with child and family learning patterns, it is also important to remember that other factors support success. When museums provide a sense of comfort by welcoming children into the new environment and creating familiar experiences, children are more successful.

Module III: Educational Theories And Theorists

Current thinking in museums reflects a constructivist approach, which suggests that knowledge is constructed within the individual and is unique to each person. A review of chapter 3 offers a foundation for group discussion, beginning with the model offered by George Hein and extending the conversation with discussion of the Early Learning Model. The brief overview of educational theorists and their ideas about cognitive development will hopefully provide new insight and meaningful connections to children's learning for some individuals or serve as a refresher for others.

Through informal conversation, participants can explore ideas related to the role of experience, play, ways of knowing, and motivation in learning, as well as include other topics of interest. Beliefs held by leading educational theorists—John Dewey, Lev Vygotsky, Jean Piaget, Maria Montessori, Jerome Bruner, Howard Gardner, and others—will broaden perspectives and build participant capacity as each individual becomes more knowledgeable about constructivist theory.

Discussion of theory is a natural extension of earlier conversations focused on characteristics of young children as learners. Ideas from educational theories shed new light on learning and offer a perspective explaining why certain practices are recommended.

Introduce the discussion by using the list of characteristics defined in the previous discussion or by using the broad statements that summarize how children learn. Simple questions will link a previous training session with a discussion on theory.

- What do educational theorists say about how children learn?
- How do their ideas relate to the group's observations about children?
- Why is theory important?

Begin with a large group discussion and then ask small groups to analyze a selected quote from one educational theorist to identify principles of learning (Appendix C). Quotations included in this module are applicable to this exercise, but there are many others readily accessible online or in original texts by theorists. Choose quotes that illuminate important ideas reflecting your museum's philosophy. As participants discuss quotes, add detail that further explains the broad concepts or principles of each theorist, particularly ideas not explicit in the quotations identified for this activity.

Encourage participants to make meaningful connections between theories and characteristics of learners. Emphasize key concepts in the discussion. For example, acknowledge the work of Jean Piaget and his emphasis on sensory learning, particularly in the early years, when the idea of children learning through their senses is raised in conversation. Another participant might comment that children observe others, interact with friends through play, and gain new ideas through conversations with teachers, family, and peers. This observation highlights the issue of learning as a social experience and is supported by Lev Vygotsky, a theorist who believed that all learning is socially mediated. Just as a reminder, Appendix C offers an overview of key concepts from selected theorists.

As educators gain insight into educational theory, they will be prepared to think about the Early Learning Model (Appendix C) introduced in chapter 3 and how it denotes behaviors or actions that define personal construction of knowledge: *explore, experience, conceptualize, imagine, create*. Encourage educators to make connections between each element of the diagram and ideas that relate to the discussion on educational theorists. Return to ELM throughout training as strategies are introduced.

It's important that participants discuss the role of theory in their work and contemplate its value. Ask small groups to respond to two key questions and then discuss as a larger group:

- Why is a theoretical framework important to early learning programming?
- How will you continue to build personal expertise in early learning theory and practice?

For many educators and interpreters, the natural inclination is to focus on *what* rather than *why* in reference to design and implementation of programs. As educators become familiar with constructivist theory and its meaning, they will more readily recognize the connections between theory and practice. Knowledge of educational theory informs practice and leads to more appropriate and effective decisions in programming.

Module IV: Object-based Learning: Every Object Tells a Story

An often-heard phrase among museum educators is that *every object tells a story*. Why is this idea so important to museums? What is its relevance to educational programming for children? This is a conversation that grounds the work of museum professionals.

Museums are places that collect, study, preserve, exhibit, and interpret objects. They are social institutions that tell stories through artifacts, scientific specimens, and works of art, sometimes relating a story about an individual object while at other times telling a story through a collection of objects that have a common theme. Discovering hidden stories, appreciating stories of the past, or learning about stories of other cultures are natural outcomes of the work of museum professionals.

But why are objects so powerful, and how can they help young children connect with the stories? By looking at a simple object, it is possible to understand the power of objects. The experience begins with careful looking or observation to be able to describe the various characteristics or defining features to reveal hidden meaning (Durbin et al. 1990). When possible, tactile experiences are important in that they provide new information that might otherwise be missed.

Each object has multiple attributes or features, but there are attributes that will be present in certain objects and not in others. For example, some objects are defined by their sentimental value—a necklace given to me by my mother—while others are not viewed in that light. Some objects are known for their function or purpose—a coffee cup—while other objects are perceived to have little purpose, such as a trinket or souvenir collected from a trip.

Most museum educators and interpreters are well aware of the adage *every object tells a story,* and yet there are many who have not given serious thought to the concept. Including this exercise in training is certainly worth the time. For many educators, this simple exercise is transformational in that it opens the mind to ways of looking at and thinking about the multiple layers of meaning and value associated with objects, and how the idea applies to objects that make up exhibitions.

In this in-depth exploration of objects, it becomes evident that objects represent more than what is obvious at first glance, but rather are powerful in what is hidden and often revealed by careful exploration. By exploring the power of objects, educators develop an increased awareness about the significance of each object and the complexity in what it represents.

Before the training, ask each participant to bring one object as an introduction: a favorite object, a family heirloom, an everyday object that marks a milestone in life, an object representing a hobby or career. There are endless categories for this exercise; choose one for the group, but emphasize the importance of the personal connections individuals have with their objects. Each person will tell the story of his object in small groups, and then the discussion leader will select a few objects to share with the large group. Sharing objects with the larger group offers an opportunity to focus attention on each object's many different characteristics and hidden meanings.

Model the process by sharing a personal object and telling its story, carefully choosing an object large enough for everyone to see. It's important to select an object that has personal value for you and communicate clearly about its meaning.

My Story
Let's look at this object together. (*My object is a ceramic thermos from China, white with a decorative royal blue motif of lotus blossoms.*) This object comes from the Nanyue King Museum in Guangzhou, China, purchased during a recent consulting trip (Figure 6.1). While it keeps my tea warm as I work at my desk, it also represents an amazing experience in a distant culture. In China I had the privilege to meet and become acquainted with museum directors and educators from the vast regions of the country and engage in conversations about constructivist learning theory, a concept quite foreign to this group of museum professionals. I now consider several new colleagues from China my friends. Every day as I drink my tea I am reminded of this unique cultural experience and all that I learned from new friends. It reminds me of my passion for museums and learning.

Figure 6.1. Chinese ceramic thermos, Guangzhou. Photo by the author.

The discussion that emerges from this exercise is one of deciphering critical attributes of each object and the meaning that is embedded within. Following the story of my ceramic thermos, the conversation would potentially include comments about the object's purpose; the concrete connection to friends, a place, and a special time; the sentimental value of the object that is irreplaceable; a reminder of a unique culture and its traditions; a strong memory of a personal experience. These are a few ideas that might arise. The discussion will not be comprehensive in nature, but will certainly cast a new light on the object. In discussions of other objects, new attributes will be showcased. In sum, it will become clear that objects hold meaning in different ways and that by thinking more deeply about each object and its story, the power of the object and possible hidden meanings will be revealed. (Appendix D provides a list of attributes that relate to objects for review after the group discussion and a guide for the gallery experience for training participants.) Plan for a similar experience in the galleries where small groups analyze an object from the collection through a focus on attributes.

Beyond the Obvious: Finding Hidden Meaning in Objects

- Objects tell **stories.**
- Objects have **meaning** that changes with the perspective of the interpreter.
- Objects have **physical attributes** (material, color, shape, size, texture, dimension, design)
- Objects have **function** or purpose.
- Objects **connect** us to people, places, and events.
- Objects have **emotional connections.**
- Objects have **value** (personal, sentimental, monetary, cultural, historical).
- Objects are **symbolic** and serve as metaphors.
- Objects **enhance memories.**
- Objects are **concrete** representations that serve as entry points for abstract ideas.

Module V: Interpretation in the Museum: Teaching Strategies

Museums tell stories through the display of objects, typically as part of a larger collection. Objects are diverse in nature, representing stories of people and events past and present, cultural traditions and rituals from around the world, scientific diversity in the natural world, and artistic expressions reflecting the human experience.

When young children visit a museum, they explore independently with family members, tour with preschool groups, or take part in programs led by facilitators that help them interpret the objects and their stories. The journey of learning is collaborative and involves a shared experience in which the discoveries of each individual are valued and important. Discussions focused on family learning allow educators to raise questions and share strategies for success and are important for guiding gallery experiences.

- How can experiences be structured so that adults and children naturally interact?
- What strategies work best to encourage collaboration between child and adult?

- How are roles defined so that adults and children understand expectations?
- What does modeling look like for adult visitors with children?
- What are the issues that arise, and how can educators deal with them with sensitivity?

There are many techniques for engaging young children and their families in galleries, but understanding how children learn and selecting techniques that are appropriate for the audience remain a priority for a successful experience.

Early Learning Strategies
Thematic Experiences—Learning to Look—Inquiry
Play—Sensory Exploration—Storytelling

Thematic Experiences

Young children make sense of their world by making associations or connections. They look for similarities and differences to identify how objects and experiences are related. This is a natural way of thinking for young children and an approach to planning that reflects theories of learning. It only makes sense that we format the museum lesson to take advantage of this natural inclination to see relationships among experiences.

Create an opportunity during professional development to explore thematic experiences. At its core is making associations by building on commonalities. A few simple exercises in classrooms or in galleries build a foundation for thinking thematically.

Making connections. Select an exhibit in the museum or create a display of carefully selected objects that have something in common—a seashell, a jar of sand, a piece of fishing net, an art print of a lighthouse—and invite participants to look closely at the objects. Set the stage for discussion with a few questions. *What do you notice about this group of objects? How are they the same and how are they different? Can you see different themes or ideas that connect all of the objects?* Certainly the objects will be recognized for their relationship to a beach or shoreline community, but with some critical thinking other commonalities will become apparent. Emerging ideas or themes are dependent upon the specific objects in the exhibition or those selected for training in the classroom.

Another collection might be objects that are made from gourds (a decorative ornament, a musical instrument, a birdhouse) or maybe a collection of objects that have decorative patterns in common (objects with geometric shapes, patterns of straight lines or triangles).

During the training session, challenge your educators with a collection that requires more critical or creative thinking to find common themes. Surprisingly, there will be multiple answers for each collection rather than one right answer. The only requirement is that the ideas need to be grounded in the evidence of the collection. The rationale has to make sense. Encouraging an open-minded approach to this exercise will more readily mimic the responses of children, who naturally see connections that adults often overlook.

Ask educators to work in pairs to analyze an existing exhibition. *Why were specific objects chosen for the exhibit? How do they contribute to the story? What objects would you add to the exhibition if you were the curator?* Making connections is part of interpreting exhibitions.

Thematic programs. Identify a theme that can be found in your museum and create a program (Appendix E: Thematic Experiences) that might be interesting to young children. Incorporate three to five objects from various exhibits, all connected by a common theme. Each object has unique characteristics and a particular story to add to the overall theme. In an art museum, almost any theme is possible and is defined by the objects selected for the program. Themes are endless and range from animals to paintings of boats to musical instruments to shapes in art. In a history museum, themes can focus on old-fashioned tools, clothing from long ago, or different modes of transportation. The museum might display Lincoln's top hat, Jackie Robinson's baseball cap, a knight's helmet, and a chef's hat as part of different exhibitions, all objects that encourage exploration of the theme of *hats*. The museum experience will be most memorable and meaningful if one theme is clearly present throughout the experience.

Interactive gallery experience. Backpacks and other family experiences designed for the museum, such as family guides, gallery games, and installed experiences, are often thematic in nature. Family packs are typically made up of simple objects, puzzles, stories, and games that have a common theme related to a work of art or an artifact in a gallery. Participants can work in small groups to design simple thematic experiences for families. Have each group select an exhibition or an artifact to explore and make a list of objects, puzzles, storybooks, and games that would complement the gallery object by connecting children and their partners to the collection.

Learning to Look

Children gather information about their world through all of their senses, but the sense of sight is one of the most powerful tools for learning. It is the ability to observe and note detail that is often the first step in building knowledge. But learning to look is more than just seeing: it is the ability to think critically about what is seen and to make connections to previous knowledge.

Looking carefully is a natural skill for young children, but can be more fully developed and honed with practice. Many of us have seen a toddler pick up a piece of lint from the floor to examine it carefully or spot a small object that no one else was able to see. The inclination to look closely is instinctive, and leveraging that interest in the visual world strengthens a child's ability to learn and make associations.

Educators are able to nurture this sense of looking using a variety of strategies. When the primary class (three- to five-year-olds) from the Palm Beach Day Academy in Florida visits the nearby Ann Norton Sculpture Gardens (Figure 6.2), they are tasked with looking closely and carefully at the sculptures

Figure 6.2. Preschoolers explore at the Ann Norton Sculpture Gardens. Photo by Courtney Ellender, Palm Beach Day Academy.

and plants in the natural environment. Armed with magnifying glasses, the children are reminded of the goal and encouraged to carefully examine the art with this simple tool. In this case, looking raises questions about the texture of the material used by the sculptor, and the children are then invited to touch to discover more about the texture. They identify other surfaces that have similar textures and describe what they feel. The process of learning begins with looking.

As educators, how do we encourage careful looking? This is an important question to pursue in training educators and gallery facilitators. Through an exercise that models the strategy of *learning to look,* new insight and techniques for developing this important skill come to light.

Begin the study of this concept of looking by using a simple, everyday object. Select a relatively large object for exploration. A shell, a feather, a branch or leaf, a decorative hat, or even a hand-crafted pot will work well. Ask an open-ended question to encourage careful looking. *What do you notice about this object?* Encourage individuals to expand their thoughts or ideas and share greater insight about the reasons behind their comments. *What makes you think that? Tell us more.*

In this exercise, let each participant examine the artifact or specimen and encourage everyone to share a discovery. *What is interesting about this object? What is most surprising to you?* Ideas will vary greatly and may include physical attributes (color, size, shape, pattern, texture, design, weight, age), associations with other objects that have similar attributes, actions for using the object, emotions or feelings about the object, or memories connected to the object. As individuals respond, extend the conversation with other questions.

For example, a large ostrich feather typically elicits a wide range of comments. Through a process of inquiry, the idea of weight becomes part of the conversation. When examining an ostrich feather, it is not uncommon for someone to mention that it is light in weight. Ideas evolve with simple questions: *What else do you know that is lightweight? What does this mean for how a feather falls to the ground? What words best describe what you think you will see? How can something big weigh so little?* Each question builds on previous statements and at the same time inspires thought about new ideas. Being open to experimentation engages the educator or the visitor in questioning, making predictions, thinking critically, and observing outcomes.

In the gallery, the looking might begin with an artifact on display or with a teaching object such as the ostrich feather that serves as an entry point for an object in the collection. When looking at Audubon prints of birds, a feather is a natural entry point for thinking about the art. The object brings the visual experience of the art to life, adds detail, and makes the experience personal for children. With inquiry as the basis of exploration, knowledge is constructed collectively and individually.

Looking doesn't stand alone, but becomes a richer experience when coupled with other strategies or techniques. In the case of the ostrich feather, looking and inquiry are strategies that complement one another and allow deeper understanding.

While it is possible to focus on one object when looking, learning can be enriched by a comparison of objects. This makes sense in light of what we know about young children. They are astute observers and notice similarities and differences with ease. Their ability to discriminate based on attributes leads to sorting, ordering, and classifying, and ultimately making judgments about the world and what it means.

The *learning to look* experience can be more fully developed when a second object becomes part of the exploration. Invite educators and interpreters to look carefully at two objects and then compare, identifying similarities and differences (Appendix E: Learning to Look). Choose two objects that have common traits and yet are distinct in some manner: a peacock feather and an ostrich feather; a rose and a daisy; a silver teapot and a handcrafted folk art teapot; a fern and a maple leaf; a conch shell and a cockle shell; an African headrest and a ceramic pillow from Asia. This exercise works well in the classroom or the galleries. Ideas are endless and can reflect your collection, or can be everyday objects that are easy to find.

Notice that a comparison encourages more careful looking and attention to detail. *What features do the peacock feather and the ostrich feather have in common? Are the edges that define the shape of leaves the same or different: sharp or rounded, flat or curled? Are the design patterns of shells similar, or do they have characteristics that distinguish one from another?* Comparing draws attention to specific detail within an object and serves as an entry point for looking more closely at a second object.

Learning to Look with Educators

Educators examine an artifact, like an African headrest, where there is an opportunity to have a personal connection to the object and to share perspectives within the group. Ask participants to look carefully at the artifact and share observations. *What did we learn from looking closely at this object?* After looking carefully, encourage each person to think about the evidence that supports his interpretation. *Why do you think that?* Throughout the conversation, questions will be raised by the discussion leader and educators engaged in the experience. *How is this object used? Why was it created? Who might use this headrest? What does the ornate design tell us about the owner? What would it feel like to exchange our familiar pillow with the unfamiliar headrest?* Constructing meaning becomes a social experience that is collaborative in nature. It also allows for experimentation where ideas are tested, not simply discussed. Meaning develops or is constructed as each individual integrates new experiences with prior knowledge.

Drawing. Another technique that heightens awareness of detail is *drawing*. Introduce the concept of drawing, in the classroom or in the gallery, and ask participants to think about the value of this technique. Set the stage by placing an object on each table in the classroom or venture into the gallery to a carefully selected object or exhibition. For example, a collection of Native American clay pots are likely distinct in their design and shape. Drawing one pot with a unique design encourages increased attention with an emphasis on the shape and the lines creating the design.

Discussion about drawing in the gallery leads to greater appreciation and understanding of the value of this technique.

- How does this experience change the way that you look?
- What are the benefits for using drawing in the gallery?
- What artifacts or exhibitions are most suited to this technique?

It is helpful to remind everyone that preschoolers and kindergartners are developing fine motor skills during this stage of growth, and that each child develops at his or her own pace. For children with less-developed skills, drawing might be less appealing. For slightly older children with more refined skills, drawing can be an effective tool for gallery experiences. Aligning strategies with the abilities and learning style of young visitors is ultimately most important for a successful museum experience.

Inquiry

Inquiry is defined as seeking truth, information, or knowledge through a process of questioning and is often thought about in relationship to the Socratic Method. The process of inquiry in a museum setting engages children, or for that matter any visitor, in investigation, questioning, examination, and exploration. It is a social process in which discoveries by individuals within the group contribute to collaborative learning. In light of Vygotsky's work on learning and his belief that "every function in a child's cultural development appears twice; first on the social level, and later, on the individual level" (Vygotsky 1978, p. 57), an inquiry-based approach is a wise choice for engaging children and families in museums and is likely to lead to increased learning and shared meaning making.

With this approach, educators ask open-ended questions to begin the exploration and then listen carefully to the responses (Figure 6.3). The questioning strategy used with the ostrich feather exemplifies the process of inquiry and shows what it looks like in practice. Pose an open-ended question, listen carefully to responses, and then extend the conversation with a question that is connected to the response. Listening is a critical skill when facilitating an inquiry-based experience. The discussion develops from the ideas and insights expressed by the children, but can also be redirected by

Figure 6.3. Inquiry-based discussion in the art gallery. Photo courtesy of Maha alEssa.

the educator through a question that encourages thoughtful responses about the artwork or exhibit that was unnoticed.

There are a variety of inquiry-based strategies in the field, each serving different purposes. Thinking Routines, created by Harvard's Project Zero, offer a simple approach to questioning that works well with young children. As mentioned earlier, a favorite routine is "I See, I Think, I Wonder." Other routines such as "Think/Puzzle/Explore," "Beginning/Middle/End," and "Circle of Viewpoints" are all interesting possibilities that encourage ways of looking. Responses lead to interesting discussions guided by the teacher or museum educator. Project Zero's Thinking routines (see chapter 5) emphasize making thinking visible through a structured process of looking and questioning.

Educators will develop skills and confidence through experience and modeling of inquiry. Model the process using an object of interest. Ask participants to share their observations and insights gleaned from the exercise prior to asking small groups to practice the technique. For this practice session, provide a selection of objects—art reproductions, cultural artifacts, specimens from nature—or go into the galleries. Individuals within small groups should be encouraged to take turns leading inquiry-based discussions focused on one artifact, specimen, or artwork. Ask everyone to note challenges, successes, and questions about the process for a follow-up discussion.

Play: A Child's Work

Much has been written about play as a *child's work*, a quote attributed to Piaget ([1951] 1962). Theorists identify play as a child's natural way of learning and recognize value in this approach to meaning making (review "Play" in chapter 3). There are many different types of play and opportunities for introducing this strategy into gallery experiences for young museum visitors.

For young children, there is often a fine line separating reality and fantasy. Children are easily transported between the real world and a place that functions in a different way. As one preschooler visits the National Postal Museum in Washington, DC, with his class, he quickly develops a personal relationship with Owney, a small dog who gained fame as the mascot for the Railway Mail Service when he traveled across the country on mail trains (Figure 6.4). This preschooler's connection to Owney is evident in the way he greets his newfound friend and later when he waves goodbye before leaving the gallery, an act that has meaning in the real world but also is important in the child's imaginative world. In play, the lines are often blurred.

It's important to make a connection between the objects in the gallery and a child's experience. With a little thought, this is relatively easy to do. In the training session (Appendix E: Play), share several examples that represent possibilities from other museums as well as from your own gallery. For example, young children love to enjoy special treats. They are also intrigued by the process of baking, an experience that is familiar at home, when visiting relatives, and possibly in the community. A trip to a bakery is likely familiar to many children. Introduce the painting *Cakes* by Wayne Thiebaud from the National Gallery of Art—or a similar painting from your museum—and think about playful ways for children to connect with the concept of baking. How can we encourage our young museum visitors to use their imaginative powers: to pretend to be a chef, a baker, someone shopping at the bakery? Would props—an icing bag with decorative tips, a bowl and spatula, a baker's hat—add to the experience? Can children step into the role of a baker and decorate construction paper shapes representing cakes using pieces of yarn or small cut-out shapes? Simple props that are safe for galleries add to the experience.

In imaginative play, children take on the roles they observe in their world and reinterpret what they see. This tie to prior knowledge is evident in how children take on the role of baker when viewing *Cakes*. Personal experiences

Figure 6.4. Imaginative play at the National Postal Museum: greeting a new-found friend. Photo by Sarah Erdman.

inform a child's play and also contribute to the learning of peers as children collectively negotiate meaning in play. Vygotsky's concept of *scaffolding* is most often associated with adults providing support for learning, but in play it is often a more knowledgeable peer who offers the necessary scaffolding for the less-experienced child.

Play is an effective strategy for interpreting historical or cultural artifacts. Consider a ceremonial crown or robe on display in an exhibition. This is a time to encourage children to imagine wearing the crown. *Who would wear it? What would it feel like? How does the crown or robe make you feel special? What do you wear that makes you feel special?*

Identifying potential scenarios for play requires adults to suspend reality and think beyond the artificial parameters that so neatly define how they see the world. Take a walk through the galleries and think about possible character roles for dramatic interpretation or in the case of the art museum look to the artist as the inspiration.

Krakowski provides a great example of play in the art museum. In "Museum Superheroes" (Krakowski 2012, p. 55–56), she describes the fanciful experience of kindergartners becoming superheroes at the Warhol Museum in Pittsburgh, and how their cape making and roleplay served as an interpretive strategy for connecting to Warhol's works of art. Long after the museum experience, the children were easily able to recall details of their day of play at the Warhol Museum and the paintings they saw.

Young children show unbridled enthusiasm for even simple activities based in imaginative play. While looking at sculpture with a group of young visitors, invite them to become the sculptor and imagine using special tools to shape the marble or weld the steel in a fashion that mimics the actions of the artist. This type of activity captures the imagination and engages the children in an active role while looking at and talking about the artwork.

It's important to note that setting parameters for behavior before the museum experience, albeit with positive words and tone, sets the stage for appropriate museum etiquette. Let your young visitors know that you trust them to maintain the safety of the artworks or artifacts through their actions. Ask the children to suggest rules that they think are appropriate. They might surprise you with their wisdom!

In a history museum, you might consider playful experiences that relate to an exhibition of antique bicycles. At the Smithsonian's National Museum of American History, one past exhibition displayed bicycles from many eras, which held great appeal to young visitors. Children were asked to imagine riding one of the old-fashioned bicycles and encouraged to think about how difficult it might be to reach the pedals or balance on such a small seat. They were invited to join in a *pretend* bicycle race. The educator modeled the motion of pedaling the bike by moving while standing in place or by sitting on the floor and narrated the imaginary journey over hills and through parks, returning to the exhibition after a long ride. Storytelling became an important part of this play scenario.

Some museums offer an opportunity to step on to an old-time trolley, a bus, or a train to take a pretend trip. Not only will children take on the role of passenger, but the gallery interpreter can also take on a role, possibly driver or conductor. The context is established and the children furnish the imagination with just a little guidance.

The Skirball Cultural Center in Los Angeles offers another notable example of play in the gallery. In this case, the play experience is built into the exhibition. Children enjoy the animals crafted from found objects, become Noah or a keeper of the animals on Noah's ark, experience the storms rocking the ship, or pretend to be one of the animals. Through play, children and adults alike are drawn into the experience and the story of Noah.

Children's museums are truly the experts in designing exhibitions that tap into the natural love of play. There are many exhibitions that honor play and its role in the lives of children. *Playscape* at the Children's Museum of Indianapolis was designed as an environment created for exploration for little ones under the age of five. Children become musicians playing authentic instruments, or take on the role of explorer to make new discoveries in the underwater habitat. At the Portland Children's Museum in Oregon, exhibitions differ in content but invariably include play. Children have the option to take part in water play, explore light and shadow, take the stage for a theater production, or grab a tool belt and hardhat to join in construction. In the realm of play and sensory experience, children's museums are wonderful models and potentially serve as a catalyst for bringing play into traditional museums.

Ideas related to play are endless. Sharing engaging examples of play during training for the education staff will hopefully open their minds to the possibilities and build a foundation for thinking about play in their museums. There are few strategies more effective for little ones than channeling their imaginative powers when visiting a gallery.

Sensory Exploration

The senses—sight, sound, taste, touch, and smell—are essential for learning, particularly for young children, and museums are places where sensory experiences abound. Sight is perhaps the most prominent sensory experience in museums, evident in visual displays that are thoughtfully designed to capture the imagination and draw visitors into new places for discovery. This rich visual environment appeals to everyone, but particularly to little ones. Think about the *I Spy* books authored by Jean Marzollo that captivate and hold the attention of young children. The museum offers a similar opportunity, only in real life.

Theorist Jean Piaget recognized that the senses play a critical role in learning from the earliest days of life and even named the initial phase of development the Sensorimotor Stage. Maria Montessori also saw learning in relationship to the senses and crafted unique sensorial materials to enhance the process of learning. The senses are an essential element of experiential learning (review chapter 3).

In today's world of museums, exhibitions are not merely visual experiences; in many cases they engage visitors through sound and touch, and at times, even smell. Animals roar, thunder booms, and the lights flash in the midst of the storm in the Smithsonian's Hall of Mammals at the National Museum of Natural History. George Washington's Mount Vernon offers an immersive theater experience in which snowflakes fall on visitors and cannons roar to make the crossing of the Delaware an experience rather than a page in a history book. A current exhibit on woven baskets is now likely to have touchable fibers for visitors to feel as well as opportunities to experiment with the process of weaving. It is not just about looking. More and more, designers are adding sensory dimensions to exhibitions to bring the stories to life.

For exhibitions that focus primarily on the visual experience, educators can add other sensory-rich elements that will engage children more fully. A sense of touch adds a meaningful dimension to almost any gallery experience and can easily be implemented with a collection of teaching objects that visitors can explore. The teaching collection can be composed of objects designated by the museum for this purpose, or it can include everyday objects found easily in the community. Family backpacks or child-friendly installations in galleries may also add this sense to the encounter with artifacts or works of art. The goal is to extend the visitor's experience beyond the visual to connect with the content and mood of the exhibit through other senses.

Engaging the senses is a strategy easily introduced in educator and docent training sessions. Share some examples and then immerse training participants in brainstorming possible ideas related to classroom artifacts and art reproductions before venturing into the gallery to consider opportunities for enhanced sensory experience in an educational program.

One effective gallery strategy is to link a small collection of objects to the artifacts in the exhibition. At the Bishop Museum in Honolulu, imagine a children's program that begins with a walk through Hawaiian Hall with a small basket of carefully selected objects from nature. Each object offers a tangible connection to the stories within the exhibitions. Many cultural artifacts on display in Hawaiian Hall were made from natural materials, such as plant fibers, rocks, gourds, feathers, shells, shark teeth: objects represented in the basket. With a collection of these natural materials, children can connect each artifact on display with its origins. The beautiful feathered capes of high-ranking members of society were made with the golden feathers of a rare bird. Containers for carrying water as well as musical instruments crafted from dried gourds gain new meaning when connected to the fresh gourds from the garden. Children gain new insight into the museum's collection by touching simple objects in the basket, such as a golden feather, or perhaps a fresh gourd. These tactile experiences lead to rich conversations about the collections as children make connections between the artifacts on display and objects they can touch.

Touchable objects related to a specific painting or exhibition can serve as a provocation. A cello string and a cotton string are perfect objects to encourage children to think deeply about a concept. *What is a string? Are all strings the same? How are strings used?* These questions invoke connections to past experience for the children and at the same time serve as a beginning point for exploring *The Cellist* by Chaim Soutine, a painting at The McNay Art Museum in San Antonio, Texas. In comparing the cello string with the cotton string, children will notice similarities and differences. Delving more deeply into the reasons for the differences enriches the experience and broadens children's perspectives.

Think about a portrait gallery, not always a place considered friendly to preschoolers. And yet, with the addition of sensory-rich techniques, portraits become more engaging. There are stories embedded within portraits that become real through the use of teaching objects. As children look at a seventeenth-century portrait of a woman, the conversation takes on new meaning with a tactile experience of different swatches of fabric that relate in some way to the painting. Touching a sample of lace encourages children to look at the stiff, ruffled lace collar with new perspective and imagine the feeling of wearing a collar made from the lace. The sensory experience changes the looking.

Another painting well suited to this strategy is Degas' *Dancers at the Old Opera House* (National Gallery of Art, Washington, DC). When children feel the velvet similar to the heavy stage curtains, or explore the texture of tulle often used for the ballerina's tutu, the painting comes to life.

Other objects found in paintings encourage careful looking as well as connect to prior knowledge for children. An artist's palette, along with some brushes, is an introduction to an artist's self-portrait. *Why is the man in the painting holding the artist's palette and brushes?* A ball begins a discussion about children playing a game of cricket. *What game are the children playing with that ball?* The object allows for a tactile experience related to the artifact or work of art, which in turn encourages careful looking at the museum artifact on display.

Encourage educators to experiment with sensory experiences (Appendix E: Sensory Exploration) and identify opportunities to expand learning by tapping into sight, sound, taste, touch, and smell. Possibilities are endless. Educators can add sound to a painting with a tape recording of music or with a musical instrument, play a classical ballet composition to give context to a Degas painting, or use drumsticks to make the sound of a marching band. A simple scent of cinnamon or vanilla can invoke a memory of baking

126

cakes while the cold, hard texture of granite offers new information about the stone used to create a favorite sculpture. The scent from a small spice container will not be harmful in the gallery, but will enhance the experience if it relates to the exhibition. In the museum world, where touching is not often possible, employing strategies that include the senses adds a new dimension to museum visits that is particularly appropriate for the learning style of young visitors.

Storytelling

The concept of storytelling is central to museums and also a familiar activity in the lives of young children. For most museums, objects are critical in telling the stories of people, places, events, and times. In fact, museums are often defined by their collections and stories of objects. Storytelling also holds a special place in the lives of children. It is through storytelling or narrative that they learn and ultimately interpret their world.

Storytelling through children's books holds a prominent place in early childhood education. The children's book market has seen unimaginable growth since the 1980s, and today offers parents and teachers opportunities to explore ideas and encourage imagination in a way that was unparalleled in the past. Storytelling is an accepted method of teaching and aligns with ways that children naturally connect with their world. It is a technique that makes sense for museum programming for young learners.

In looking back at the previous strategies, it's clear that there is an intersection of techniques, and that one is often coupled with another. In a thematic program, the main idea is carefully selected for choosing artifacts or works of art. A high-quality children's book enriches the overall experience and typically extends ideas within the program.

At the Amricani Cultural Center in Kuwait, children and their companions are fascinated by the Markhor goat, notable for its curly horns and elaborate candelabra (Figure 6.5). A perfect introduction to the artifact is the tale of the Three Billy Goats Gruff. Stephen Carpenter's version of the story (1998) provides a framework for discussion where the children think about which billy goat in the story is most like the Markhor goat in the gallery. *Is it the youngest billy goat, the first to cross the bridge, the middle billy goat, or the biggest billy goat?* As children debate, they are asked to justify their thinking. *Why do you think that?* The conversation continues with looking at the Markhor goat and comparing the features with one of the goats from the story. *How are the goats the same? How are they different?* As the children make comparisons, they look more closely at the artifact and the images in the book. The story grounds the museum experience for young children already comfortable with this type of activity.

During a training session, think about themes represented by exhibitions in your museum (Appendix E: Storytelling); select one theme and then

Figure 6.5. Markhor goat. © The al-Sabah Collection, Dar al-Athar al-Islamiyyah, Kuwait.

search for the perfect book. The vast array of books across every imaginable topic means that there is a children's book for every possible museum theme, from Mexican pottery to the shearing of sheep. In today's world, the Web provides access to titles of children's books linked to themes or topics. The important decision is in finding a high-quality, age-appropriate book that supports the exhibition and offers an interesting introduction or expansion of ideas from the exhibit. Caldecott Award winners are high-quality children's books and a perfect place to begin your search.

For a botanic garden or horticulture exhibit, look at *Tree is Nice* by Janice May Udry (1987); examine *Freight Train* by Donald Crews (2011) for a train exhibition; for an exhibit about animals, look at *What Do You Do With a Tail Like This?* by Steve Jenkins and Robin Page (2003); review *Swirl by Swirl* by Joyce Sidman (2011) to go with a shell exhibit. There are literally thousands of choices to look at online, at the bookstore, or by visiting your local library.

Look for children's books that are rich in sensory language and relate to the content of the exhibition. Authors use words and illustrations to bring life to ideas, from portraying sounds of a railroad crossing or the luscious taste of an ice cream sundae to words of a lullaby or the description of the feel of sand on your toes at the ocean.

Reading children's books is only one approach to storytelling. Telling a story is qualitatively different from reading a story. It is often more dramatic than reading a book and incorporates various gestures, voice, and characterization. The story comes to life when the storyteller assumes a role with costume, gesture, and vocal qualities of a character portrayed in the story. Folk tales like those about the spider trickster Anansi are great for storytelling and fit well with spider sculptures by Louise Bourgeois. Storytelling is also a perfect addition to a historical art series such as *Harriet Tubman* or *The Migration* by Jacob Lawrence. The inclusion of narrative, whether through children's books or storytelling, resonates with young children and supports meaning making.

Conclusion

Today's museums are embracing young children and learning from best practice in the field of early childhood education as well as from children's museums. And while the passion and commitment continues to grow, there are also questions and concerns about how to best serve this audience. The answers lie in research, model programs, and experience garnered by educators dedicated to early learning.

The ideal is to create a place where children and families are welcome and where opportunities exist to engage, excite, and inspire learning. It is essential that museum professionals recognize the defining features of young children and incorporate appropriate strategies when planning museum experiences for this audience. Aligning theory and practice is the underpinning for a strong program. For that reason, an important component of any training session on strategies is discussion about why the strategy makes sense for this audience. What does theory say that is supported by this strategy? How does the strategy make sense based upon what we know about the learning style of young children? Building background knowledge within the museum staff and honoring the learning style of young children will contribute to the quality of programs and exhibits that museums develop.

Museums have much to offer young children and families, but they are just beginning to tap into the possibilities for creating quality experiences for early learners. As museum professionals look to the future, the vision begins with promising practices of today. What are experts saying about successful practices today? What is on the horizon for early learning in museums? What changes can we anticipate? What are our hopes? While the answers are not yet clear, it is a time of excitement for early learning in museums as we look forward and consider the possibilities.

Making a Difference:
The Promise of the Future

CHAPTER SEVEN

Making a Difference: The Promise of the Future

"There is always one moment in childhood when the door opens and lets the future in."

—*Graham Greene*

Introduction

Museums are places that delight, inspire, and intrigue. For decades, the magic of museums has fascinated educators interested in unleashing the imagination of the child. This idea is present in the time-honored publication *Museums, Magic & Children,* in which the opening describes the child's experience as "the magic transformation that occurs when children learn from exhibitions and objects in the collections of museums" (Pitman-Gelles 1981, p. 5). We can thank those advocates and all that came before them for advancing the cause of young children across the museum community.

Today, magical experiences continue to open the minds of the young to the many wonders of the world. Museums offer young visitors a chance to experience something new, such as seeing musical instruments from ancient cultures, or explore more deeply an existing passion. A moment that changes the future for a young child might be an encounter with a paleontologist explaining how scientists discovered and now study fossils from long ago, a hands-on experience in a children's museum that encourages thinking about cause and effect, or a visit to the art museum where the beauty of a work of art captures a child's imagination. That moment in time, no matter how precious and memorable, might go unnoticed by everyone except the child, but it might be a moment that changes the future.

Today's growing enthusiasm for young children within museums represents society's twenty-first century commitment to this audience and recognition of the value of early learning experiences. Nationally and internationally, we are celebrating the opening of new programs that expand museum experiences to include younger children. In Kuwait, the Amricani Cultural Center (ACC) is now touching the lives of little ones through a monthly story time for toddlers and by expanding the children's

Engaging Young Children in Museums, by Sharon E. Shaffer, 133–154. © 2015 Left Coast Press, Inc. All rights reserved.

art workshop series to introduce preschoolers to art and culture through art making and gallery walks. At the Barnes Foundation in Philadelphia, underserved preschoolers in Head Start programs are learning to look at art and make connections to their world through paintings and sculpture from the Barnes collection. Dr. Barnes' concept of the ensemble, once reserved for more sophisticated students of visual arts, is now a familiar topic of conversation for these youngsters. Preschoolers at the Bishop Museum in Honolulu explore cultural concepts through artifacts in Hawaiian Hall and learn through interactive, multisensory programs. The children enjoying these experiences are privileged, not by wealth or status, but by the opportunities to learn about their world through art and artifacts in museums. They are seeing the world through authentic objects that tell important stories rather than simply learning about these stories from books.

As we know, research suggests that positive museum experiences early in life are likely to lead to a meaningful relationship with museums and create a bond for the future (Carr 1999; Piscitelli and Anderson 2000). In that way, the benefits associated with early learning programs in museums appear to have a long-lasting impact, not only for the child but also potentially in shaping patrons for the future.

As we ponder the promising practices in museums today and consider the possibilities of what the future might hold, we begin by opening our minds to ideas from the field. To arrive at this understanding of promising practice based on current trends and a vision for the future, I informally surveyed and interviewed a select group of national and international museum professionals and educators connected to traditional art, science, history, and cultural institutions; children's museums; and schools (see "Survey Participants"). I then analyzed the responses, much like a qualitative study, looking for common ideas to define trends. All respondents are passionate about young children and the potential for learning in museums. From experts in early learning research in museums to professionals dedicated to serving preschoolers and younger audiences, there is a shared vision for expanding the role of museums in the lives of children.

Promising Practice and a Vision for the Future
Trend I: Seeing Value in Early Learning in Museums: Almost There

Many museums across the nation see young visitors as a valuable audience and recognize the potential for creating rich learning experiences in galleries. But this has not always been the case: today, it is not unusual to see preschoolers engaged in meaningful experiences in historic homes, art museums, science centers, or cultural institutions, whereas this was far less common before the turn of the twenty-first century. Not only are children

Survey Participants
Göran Björnberg, Global Perspectives Analyst, Swedish Exhibition Agency
Kathy Danko-McGhee, Toledo Museum Of Art, Emma Leah Bippus
Director Of Education
Susan Day, Dar al-Athar al-Islamiyyah (DAI)
Education Consultant, Amricani Cultural Center, Kuwait
Jo Graham, Early Learning Specialist And Consultant, United Kingdom
Kimberlee Kiehl, Executive Director, Smithsonian Early Enrichment Center
Pamela Krakowski, Clinical Assistant Professor, University Of Pittsburgh
Ted Lind, Retired Deputy Director Of Education, Newark Museum (2007–2013)
Bonnie Pitman, Distinguished Scholar In Residence/Co-Director Center For
Interdisciplinary Study Of Museums At The University Of Texas At Dallas
Donna Tobey, Head of Lower School, Palm Beach Day Academy, Florida
Jeanne Vergeront, Director, Vergeront Museum Planning, Minneapolis

present in today's museums, but many of these institutions are acknowledging the value or benefits reaped from the encounters.

As a leader in the field, the Smithsonian Institution recognizes the value of early learning and reflects that belief in a commitment found in programs across the organization. The Institution's newest museum now under construction, The National Museum of African American History and Culture (NMAAHC), has dedicated assets to early learning and is establishing a Center for African American Resources on Early Education even before the museum's anticipated opening in 2015. This investment in the young is worth the time and effort; according to NMAAHC Education Specialist Anna Forgerson Hindley, it is in place to support the museum's lofty goal to influence society and make the world a better place.

Firmly ensconced within the Smithsonian culture is the National Museum of American History [NMAH]. With the 2015 opening of its new education center, the museum will cater to museumgoers aged five and under in a hands-on, experiential space for learning through play and exploration. The environment will incorporate displays of real artifacts and provide interactive experiences to encourage thoughtful connections to the real world. A tugboat structure for climbing will serve as a landmark object, modeled after an artifact in the museum. A replica of the Smithsonian's clock tower in the castle offers yet another opportunity for learning. According to Sarah Erdman, the Goldman Sachs Fellow for Early Learning at NMAH, the space is a place of learning not only for children but also for parents and caregivers. One goal is to create a sense of comfort and build confidence for adults to make the leap from playful exploration to discovery experiences in the galleries. Stories from the collection will be highlighted in the children's space as little ones are introduced to the concept of collections and why each object is special.

The Smithsonian's National Air and Space Museum set the tone for early learning by employing "the first museum educators specifically dedicated to early childhood audiences in the Smithsonian," according to Ann Caspari, Early Childhood Education Specialist. At the museum preschoolers enjoy *Flights of Fancy,* stories for children, and learn about the night sky in *One World, One Sky,* a planetarium program designed with preschoolers in mind. Early learning at the museum is generously supported by the Conrad N. Hilton Foundation, which gave $10 million to establish the Barron Hilton Endowed Fund, a source reserved primarily for early childhood education. In fact, the endowment funded a redesign of the *Pioneers of Flight* exhibition, which incorporates child-friendly components to engage younger learners.

Other well-respected cultural institutions show similar interest and commitment to young children. The Metropolitan Museum of Art offers story time programs for toddlers as well as preschool experiences for looking at art, encouraging young museumgoers to look, sketch, and listen to stories as they explore works of art. The Phipps Conservatory and Botanical Gardens in Pittsburgh reaches out to preschoolers through camps, story time, and gallery programs that build awareness about nature and science through participatory experiences. The Chicago History Museum reports huge popularity for *Crazy for Trains,* a program that supports preschoolers as they explore trains through dramatic play, stories and poetry, and building activities. These are simply a few examples from today's museums.

And while early learning seems to be flourishing and can be identified as a promising trend, consultant Jeanne Vergeront, director of Vergeront Museum Planning in Minneapolis, suggests that when compared with children's museums where the belief of inherent value is field-wide, "in art, science, and history museums, this recognition has been institution specific" (J. Vergeront, February 7, 2014). She believes that "in the best of circumstances, museums are now viewing children as capable and competent learners and interested museum-goers" (J. Vergeront, February 7, 2014), but recognizes that this is not universally accepted. In her view, the increase in programming for young children is in part driven by the understanding that children have the capacity to learn and benefit from their experience in museums.

Ted Lind, retired Deputy Director for Education at the Newark Museum (2007–2013), joins Vergeront in applauding this increased interest in young museumgoers and defines the value for children when he suggests that "the collections of art museums present a wider view of the world for young learners—seeing other times and places that are beyond their own neighborhoods and limited environments" (T. Lind, February 10, 2014). The decision made by museums to be more inclusive and welcome younger visitors goes beyond the desire to expand the diversity of their audience, but is embedded in a belief that there is value inherent in the child's experience.

In recent years, our view of early learning has taken on new meaning. While the initiative was once viewed as extending museum experiences to preschoolers, museum professionals now see opportunities to engage babies and toddlers. Our worldview is changing with the influx of new technology and brain research.

Kathy Danko-McGhee recently wrote about the value of gallery tours or programs for babies and toddlers and the research that supports the initiative (Danko-McGhee 2013). In her role as Director of Education at the Toledo Museum of Art, Danko-McGhee documents the attention and interaction of little ones in art galleries, detailing the engagement during gallery tours. Programs are based on the belief that early stimulation in the form of looking at and interacting with art enhances visual literacy (Danko-McGhee 2013). Educators and docents engaging the young visitors and their adult counterparts are "trained in the neuroscience of early brain growth and development" (Danko-McGhee 2013, p. 52), an approach grounded in research. Technological advances further studies at places such as the Institute of Learning and Brain Sciences at the University of Washington in Seattle, where researchers examine the impact of early experiences on the neurological development of the brain (Reddy 2013). In addition to enhancing visual literacy, early experiences are prime opportunities for language development and reasoning, particularly when babies are immersed in rich vocabulary through interactions with their parent or caretaker.

And while the Toledo Museum of Art may be out front in this effort, particularly in the area of research, others around the nation and on the international stage are also investing in building gallery experiences for this very young audience. The Leigh Yawkey Woodson Art Museum in Wausau, Wisconsin, is one of those institutions that designs unique experiences for little ones from *Art Babies* and *Art Time for Tots* to *Toddler Tuesdays* for the museum's youngest visitors. The Chicago History Museum is also going beyond the preschool experience, testing stroller tours for little ones. This inclusion of babies, while relatively new in the United States, is gaining traction in the United Kingdom.

Lending an international perspective to this conversation is Jo Graham, an early learning specialist and museum consultant from England. She provides insight into the current state of early learning in the United Kingdom, recounting a significant shift in museums' perceptions of early learners. According to Graham, the initial movement in the United Kingdom, starting in the 1990s, forged a path for preschoolers in museums, whereas more recent innovation in practice focuses on babies and toddlers.

Graham notes that it is only in the past 20 years that permanent galleries have become part of the fabric of museums in the United Kingdom for children younger than six, marking the beginning of this group as a core audience, and that today "early years are seen as a standard, if challenging, part of general audiences for many museums and galleries in England" (J. Graham, March 12, 2014), with dedicated spaces such as *Curiosity* at Bristol City Museum and *Little Liverpool* at the Museum of Liverpool, or interactive areas with appeal for early years such as the Science Museum in London. In fact, there are some who tout the Science Museum for its early experiments in early learning well before the latest trend. According to Graham, the Science Museum had a Children's Gallery as well as Launch Pad, a science center that can be categorized as an interactive gallery, but neither "was exclusively focused on early years" (J. Graham, March 12, 2014), although of course young children were drawn to the space. Beyond dedicated spaces, Graham notes that national and regional museums are also offering the young visitor gallery experiences through specially designed programs. Graham ascribes this interest by museums in England to recognizing the value of early years' audiences as loyal, lifelong visitors (J. Graham, March 12, 2014).

This interest in babies is also evident in other countries. At the Museu Internacional De Arte Naif Do Brasil in Rio de Janeiro, infants and their caregivers are making connections to paintings through visual and tactile experiences as they play with colored scarves and feathers. In one gallery, babies and toddlers join visitors of all ages in unique sensorial experiences where touching the art is expected and encouraged. Paintings and sculpture are created specifically for this personal encounter with texture. As time passes, opportunities are expanding for young museum visitors as more and more museums design unique opportunities for preschoolers and their younger counterparts.

Göran Björnberg, a global perspectives analyst with the Swedish Exhibition Agency, greets this trend with enthusiasm. As a long-time advocate of early learning, Björnberg sees the influx of young visitors to museums as an important trend and makes a case for identifying young children in museums as "a target group which [*sic*] needs to be taken seriously and professionally" (G. Björnberg, April 6, 2014). With this promise to younger visitors comes a commitment to what Björnberg calls "professionalization of pedagogical activities and programs in museums," which he sees as a consequence of this dedication to the audience (G. Björnberg, April 6, 2014). This professionalization requires educators, curators, and exhibition designers to be knowledgeable in theory and pedagogy related to young children and able to discriminate differences between the various age groups that fall within the broad category of *children*.

This sentiment resonates with Kimberlee Kiehl, Executive Director for the Smithsonian Early Enrichment Center, and is evident as she reflects on current practice. Her experience indicates that "educators are being more thoughtful about developing experiences for young children that go beyond free play but still are playful in nature and developmentally appropriate" (K. Kiehl, May 5, 2014). Kiehl suggests that it is time to present "children with real experiences and real objects" and to respect "young children as being capable of carefully observing, asking questions, and searching for knowledge" in their encounters in galleries or in classrooms (K. Kiehl, May 5, 2014).

Almost without exception, the educational leaders I surveyed see a transformation in the perception of young children as museum visitors and increased understanding of the value of the museum experience in early learning. This positive change marks a strategic milestone for envisioning the future of early learning in museums.

Our twenty-first century vision reframes the notion of early learning from site-specific places embracing younger learners to a conversation about universal support for and interest in young children within the museum community. It also expands our thinking about the artificial boundaries used in the past to define early learning and now broadens our definition to include babies and toddlers. The future revolves around viewing members of this audience with full understanding of their capacity to learn and grow through interactions with collections while at the same time recognizing opportunities within the museum's framework that add a new dimension to learning not found in other settings.

Trend II: Engaging the Senses: Connecting Mind, Body, and Spirit

Museums have changed a great deal from the early days of static exhibit design to the interactive experiences offered in the recent past. The greatest change is evident in history and art museums, with myriad examples of exhibitions designed to include interactive elements as well as educational programs that tap into the senses. More traditional museums have clearly taken note of the success of the long-established, hands-on strategies used in science centers and children's museums. And though John Dewey espoused a need for hands-on as well as minds-on learning more than 100 years ago, it has taken a while for the museum community to fully embrace this perspective.

With the turn of the twenty-first century, museums transitioned to exhibit design and program development that included increased opportunities for sensory experience and higher levels of interaction, redefining the visitor's experience as active learning rather than passive observation. At the National Museum of Natural History in Washington, DC, visitors experience the culture of Africa's peoples by listening to music, stories, and folk tales while looking at artifacts on display. Sound stations expand the visual experience so often associated with museums in the past. Gallery spaces across America are becoming rich in sound, tactile experiences, and even scents that give meaning to exhibitions. The museum landscape is changing significantly in exhibition design by introducing sensory experiences that engage visitors in body, mind, and spirit.

Interpretation in galleries is no longer a product solely of visual experience, but rather allows individuals multiple ways to internalize and create meaning from the encounter. Howard Gardner's influence, with his belief in multiple ways of knowing, is certainly felt across the museum field and evident in institutions as they strive to reach audiences in different ways.

This shift in thinking and the innovative practice in museums appeal to young museumgoers and aligns perfectly with the way that they process and make meaning of their world. Experts surveyed unequivocally praised this inclusion of new strategies integrated into exhibition design and educational programming.

Susan Day, DAI education consultant, sees this trend at the Amricani Cultural Center (ACC) in Kuwait, where the museum follows the lead of "western museums [in] creating spaces that are inviting, interactive, and informal places of learning" (S. Day, April 30, 2014). At ACC, visitors are now asked "to explore objects, going well beyond the information on the label," which includes multisensory experiences (S. Day, April 30, 2014). According to Day, skeptics become believers once they witness the unbridled enthusiasm expressed by children as they interact with the collection.

Our experts note a range of sensory-based strategies that are becoming more familiar or prominent within museums: embodied learning, different modes of play, theater, dance, storytelling, and interactive learning. Educators embrace this change and see benefits to students. Donna Tobey, head of Lower School at Palm Beach Day Academy (PBDA) in Florida, is enthusiastic about the impact of museum experiences and recognizes the power of artifacts and collections, particularly when museums employ strategies that engage students through their senses. According to Tobey, "Rather than simply looking at pictures in a book, students can see, smell, hear, and sometimes touch real objects of significance that leave an indelible impression on them" (D. Tobey, May 13, 2014). This is why students have responded with great enthusiasm to museum field trips, and why museum–school partnerships at PBDA have been successful.

Göran Björnberg acknowledges sensory learning as a growing trend, but describes another innovative interactive strategy. He sees museums integrating what he calls *embodied learning*, where children are expressing their ideas and interpreting what they see through movement. Others in the field are supporting similar ideas. In *Museum Movement Techniques* (2006), Shelley Kruger Weisberg defines this kinesthetic approach as a valuable tool for learning. According to Weisberg, museum movement techniques provide a framework that is "based on the spatial, expressive, and social-cooperative qualities of movement" (2006, p. vii). The rationale supporting this approach, grounded in the work of Dewey and Gardner, is now becoming more commonplace in museums, with children posing like figures in paintings or sculpture and experiencing art or history kinesthetically.

Play in museums, whether children's museums or more traditional galleries, is becoming more accepted as a strategy for learning and is seen not simply as frivolous activity but the way that children construct meaning about their world. In Krakowski's article "Museum Superheroes" (2012), play takes center stage as children explore Andy Warhol's Myth series. In the galleries, kindergartners step into a make-believe world of superheroes with silk-screened capes to connect with the iconic figures captured by the artist. Play strategies were the centerpiece of this unique museum experience, creating an indelible memory for the kids involved.

Björnberg adds yet another dimension to the conversation on play. He describes a sense of freedom that comes from the imaginative meaning making that takes place during play. Accordingly, a child's sense of fantasy allows for creating narrative and filling the gaps through imagination and creative thought, free from restrictions. Björnberg cautions the field to step back at times, giving children the freedom to construct their own experience and meaning, remembering that the museum and its artifacts are simply tools or platforms that allow a child to develop his identity through social collaboration (G. Björnberg, April 6, 2014). In this conversation with early learning experts, there are differences in how they see play in the context of learning, but even with different points of view, they agree on the value of play.

The debate surrounding play has a long history and is not yet universally understood or accepted. While many give lip service to the notion that play and learning go hand in hand, behind the scenes there is often skepticism about the worth or rigor of learning through play. There is a continued need for advocacy and education for museum professionals, particularly those outside of education. For our early learning experts, though, there is no doubt about the value of play as an effective tool for learning. There is overwhelming consensus that integrating play or playful learning into museum programs adds a dimension that is worth the investment.

Other strategies, such as theater techniques and storytelling, are natural extensions of creative movement and play. Children can enter the past through storytelling and make meaningful connections to history. They can interpret what they see—in exhibitions of art, history, science, or culture—and share their ideas in a public forum.

The emphasis on hands-on, minds-on learning is found in a variety of gallery experiences. The Children's Museum in Pittsburgh redefines the role of the visitor in the *MAKESHOP* exhibition, "a space for children and families to make, play and design using "real stuff": the same materials, tools, and processes used by professional artists, builders, programmers, and creators of all kinds. It is also a place where physical materials and digital media resources intersect; where visitors are encouraged to be curious, creative, experimental and innovative" (Children's Museum Pittsburgh 2014). The interactive *MAKESHOP* experience, typically associated with science centers and children's museums, is an innovative trend that offers visitors a new dimension for exploration and learning. Museums are creating their own versions of *MAKESHOP*, usually with new exhibition titles, and redefining the experience for their visitors by the choice of materials and activities available. At first glance, this may seem useful only for museums known for their hands-on approach, but the idea is relevant for other museum types as well. Think about artists creating with found objects, and how easily this idea of *MAKESHOP* aligns with the art. As an advocate for *MAKESHOP*, Krakowski suggests that "The power of experiencing the actual object in a museum context—such as a painting, a sculpture, an historical artifact, an installation—will always have an immediacy that cannot be replaced by a reproduction in a classroom. Young children learn through using all of their senses, their bodies, their minds" (P. Krakowski, March 9, 2014).

A 2008 research action project report from the United Kingdom, *Close Encounters with Culture: Museums and Galleries as part of the Early Years Foundation Stage* (Graham 2008), echoes a similar sentiment:

> Objects, artworks and stories are a great resource for children's active learning. Whether they are incorporating them into their play, representing them, exploring them or talking about them, children can develop at their own pace and in their own way. (Graham 2008, p. 6)

According to lead investigator Jo Graham, findings indicate that through interactions with objects children strengthen their skills in investigating, communicating, representing, and recalling experiences (2008, p. 6). Objects offer new opportunities for exploration and investigation, absorbing the young visitor in learning through his senses.

We see the path we've taken to move toward active learning in museums, but the future is still undefined. Our desire to engage the child through a variety of interactive strategies is grounded in our understanding of cognitive development, but is there reason to be cautious as we continue on this path? In an ideal world, we would think about the perfect balance between experiencing the object—taking time to look carefully—and interpreting what we see through activities apart from the object in an effort to not lose sight of the object itself. Through reflective practice and evaluation, some strategies will become more prominent in programs, while others might diminish in stature. A century ago it would have been difficult to imagine the museum of today. Stretching our minds to imagine the museum of the future might be equally challenging, but a journey that we intend to travel.

Trend III: Reaching Early Learners: A Collaborative Experience

Museum education theory and practice emphasizes the importance of understanding audience. Museums typically think about *audience* in terms of visitors and differentiate audiences based on diverse characteristics of groups, a practice grounded in knowledge of cognitive development and defining attributes that represent a cross-section of the group. An audience might be defined by developmental stages or based upon special needs. In this volume, I define early learners by chronological age as well as developmental levels that exemplify a specific set of characteristics related to learning.

In recent years, the education community representing schools and museums has been examining the idea of family learning, seeing the young learner in relationship to the adults in her life. Learning as a collaborative experience is an ideal approach. As educators have embraced Lev Vygotsky's theories, the emphasis on learning as a social experience has gained acceptance in both formal and informal learning environments. This fundamental shift in thinking opens the conversation to integrally link young children to their museum partners; with that comes a focus on the social interaction that leads to increased learning. The current interest in family engagement reflects a trend toward collaborative learning, which shifts how museums think about young children and their adult partners.

Museums have a history of valuing families and supporting them with publications such as family guides. These pamphlets typically suggest ways to connect with exhibitions or works of art on display, often providing questions or other prompts as a provocation for looking, thinking, and talking about the objects or ideas and the stories they tell. Most family guides are designed for intergenerational groups, targeting school-aged children rather than preschoolers. But with some thought, many of the ideas can be adapted for younger visitors. In addition to family guides, there are specially designed spaces such as discovery rooms that foster hands-on experiences for families. Carts stationed in galleries are yet another opportunity for family interaction inspired by artifacts or natural specimens.

Young children and their families are also served through special programs, a trend showing significant growth in recent years. For example, the Walters Art Museum in Baltimore invites families to explore paintings and sculptures through ArtCarts, which are designed to enhance the family experience with children's books, drawing materials, puzzles, and costumes that relate to gallery art. Families visiting the Walters can also check out FunPacks and Discovery Quilts that offer interactive, sensory experiences for all ages. At the National Building Museum, preschoolers and their adult companions join forces to look for *Patterns: Here, There, and Everywhere!* And at the American Museum of Natural History, collections come to life in *The Early Adventures Program*, where two- to four-year-olds explore nature and science with a parent or grandparent.

In the United Kingdom, museum professionals are increasingly interested in family learning. Since parents are perceived as a child's first teacher, museums want to know how to support families in their visits to galleries.

In a collaborative project bringing together six museums, investigators and educators collected data to explore "characteristics of resources that effectively support parents as educators of pre-school children in museums and galleries" (Graham 2009, p. 3). Key findings indicate that parents are more comfortable when there is a defined mission or clear purpose for their museum activities, and seek a balance of exploration and play with choice for the family. Recommendations include "providing resources for active investigation, exploratory play, and creative expression" while also finding "family friendly ways to provide information about their collections and buildings . . . in a user-friendly format" (Graham 2009, p. 5). The report suggests that there is a need to offer playful, active learning interpretation resources for all families, to support parents in their role in museums, and to advocate to museum learning staff about the role they can play "in deepening the understanding of colleagues about the needs of families with young children" (Graham 2009, p. 5).

This concept of family learning, while not new, is gaining a newly defined status with the current research focus on scaffolding as a strategy to enhance learning. As early as 1972, parent–child workshops were breaking ground at the Metropolitan Museum of Art; although the studio component was the focus of the experience, gallery tours were also included. "In 1998, the Art Institute of Chicago received funding from The Pew Charitable Trust to launch *Looking at Art Together: Families and Lifelong Learning* to make the museum a more inviting place for families" (Clarke 2002, p. 7). Through a series of parent workshops, strategies for engaging young children with art were discussed and modeled in galleries. This initiative reflects the organization's institutional commitment and long history of investing in family programming.

Current research supports this notion of collaborative learning in which adults value interactive galleries or spaces, identifying these spaces as offering rich, sensory experiences that stimulate interesting family discussions, encourage creativity, and serve as inspiration (Adams 2011; Adams and Moussouri 2002). Research further indicates the value of parents modeling desired behaviors. In one study, Crowley and Galco (2001) suggest that parent modeling of scientific thinking in the context of gallery experience contributes to a child's understanding and learning of science. Again, according to research, it is social engagement that leads to increased learning.

Wolf and Wood (2012) examined the role of scaffolding in galleries at the Children's Museum of Indianapolis, finding that "building on simple concepts and working toward mastery of ideas can inform adults and simultaneously help children stretch to new levels of understanding and achievement" (p. 29). This study supports the notion that collaborative experience results in greater learning.

Many of our experts in the field echo this trend of viewing learning as a collaborative process. Bonnie Pitman, Distinguished Scholar in Residence/

Co-Director of the Center for Interdisciplinary Study of Museums at the University of Texas at Dallas, underscores family learning as the key to successfully engaging young children in museums (B. Pitman, interview, April 30, 2014). With her experience as the former director at the Dallas Museum of Art (DMA) and as the former director of the Bay Area Discovery Museum, Pitman developed a strong personal commitment to family learning, which became an essential element of education under her purview. Pitman credits groundbreaking efforts during the DMA's 2003 Centennial Celebration as laying the foundation for family learning. Arturo—a fun-loving parrot "whose design was based on a vessel from the ancient American collection" (DMA 2013)—was adopted as the family mascot and today welcomes visitors to the museum. Families can visit Arturo's Nest, "a relaxed learning place for children ages 4 and under and their adult companions" and "a 'please touch' space where young children can crawl, climb, and use their natural curiosity and playfulness to have early experiences with art" (DMA 2013). Late Nights—monthly evenings at the museum where activities include films, performances, gallery experiences, yoga for kids, games, stories, and more—is another example of family-friendly programming that came out of the Centennial Celebration. The Center for Creative Connections (C3) at the DMA welcomes visitors of all ages to "LOOK, TOUCH, LISTEN, READ, MAKE, and TALK about art" and be an active member of the museum community (DMA 2013).

Consultant Jeanne Vergeront reflects on the notion of families and learning, describing the role of the family and its value in the learning process. She identifies the family as a "powerful, flexible unit" that is essential for understanding children's learning (J. Vergeront, February 7, 2014). Accordingly, Vergeront states "family learning recognizes the social nature of learning [and museumgoing] and [sees] families as co-learners building on each other's knowledge and ideas" (J. Vergeront, February 7, 2014).

The Toledo Museum of Art's Baby Tours are also indicative of family learning. The gallery experience is social and structured around engaging babies with selected works of art. Parents interact with their little ones to give language to the experience by naming images and describing characteristics found within each work of art. This approach "lays the groundwork for visual, cognitive, and language development" (Danko-McGhee 2013, p. 53).

The Philadelphia Museum of Art is yet another cultural institution providing a family experience for little ones with their Baby Bird Playdates, in which adults are invited to "bring their baby birds . . . [to] enjoy a relaxed environment, circle time with music, books, and games, and the company of other art-loving adults" (Philadelphia Museum of Art 2014). Programs for infants, toddlers, and preschoolers unite children and their adult companions in the museum experience.

Family learning—with an emphasis on collaboration and interaction—deserves attention from museums. In light of current research, educators are now armed with knowledge to inform practice for engaging the family unit, either through exhibition design or public programs. In either case, family learning as a promising trend encourages museum professionals to think critically about how they engage the child and adult partner in learning.

Trend IV: Partnerships, Old and New: Reimagining and Investing

The adage that little is new in the world rings true. Rather, our way of thinking changes, with the old evolving and becoming something new as we see or redefine our ideas when looking through a different lens or imagining within a new context. When we consider the idea of partnerships, perhaps we see opportunities to collaborate in a new way, or we redefine our vision for the partnerships that existed in the past. The role of the museum or cultural institution within the community will continue to evolve, and future relationships will depend on intentional and thoughtful scripting to leverage assets in a way that benefits children.

Museum–school partnerships have existed for decades, beginning in the early days of the twentieth century and the work of progressive educators. In the 1980s and 1990s, museum–school partnerships were highlighted in field-wide journals and texts (Sheppard 1993), documented by organizations collecting data (Hirzy 1996), and studied by professionals in the field at conferences and symposiums (Science Museum of Minnesota 1996).

Many in the field credit the American Alliance of Museum's 1992 publication, *Excellence and Equity: Education and the Public Dimension of Museums,* with placing education on the center stage and shining a light on the responsibility of museums to serve the broad spectrum of society (AAM 1992). This landmark publication emphasized the museum's role of affirming fundamental principles as cited in AAM's 1984 report *Museums for a New Century* ". . . to communicate ideas, impart knowledge, encourage curiosity, and promote esthetic sensibility" (AAM 1992, p. 11). The committee's work set the stage for early learning, saying "museums have the capacity to contribute to formal and informal learning at every stage of life, from the education of children in preschool through secondary school to the continuing education of adults" (AAM 1992, p. 10).

Federally funded grants through the Department of Education were created to support innovative practice for public education by encouraging schools and museums to work together to increase student achievement and enrich learning; these grants are still awarded today. And although this conversation about partnerships between schools and museums continues today, it is time to reexamine the opportunities for making a difference in the lives of children. But where do we go from here, and how can relationships between museums and schools benefit young children in ways that go beyond the current thinking?

In the context of partnerships, our education experts propose several ideas to consider. Overwhelmingly, the experts believe that museums and schools in partnership can affect young children and their learning. Kim Kiehl envisions a future where "education is not something that is limited to what happens within four walls of a classroom somewhere, but will be something that happens across an ecosystem made of a wide variety of community assets including museums" (K. Kiehl, May 5, 2014). In this vision, there will no longer be a simplistic museum–school partnership, but a grander system that integrally links museums and early childhood programs.

Jeanne Vergeront suggests that museums become "a center for developing and advancing an evidence-based, child-centered museum pedagogy" to "develop, test, and disseminate conceptual frameworks for informal learning environments that are capable of making children's thinking and learning visible" (J. Vergeront, February 7, 2014). Centers will benefit museums and schools, thus advancing learning opportunities for young children.

Several noteworthy museum initiatives serve as models for this idea of crossing boundaries, or actually breaking down boundaries, in the area of early learning. The Bay Area Discovery Museum in California houses a Center for Childhood Creativity to provide the educational community with information about research partnerships and publications to inform practice. The Strong National Museum of Play in Rochester, New York, the only collections-based museum dedicated solely to play, seeks to contribute to the national conversation on play through its exhibitions, programs, and publications. The Strong's *American Journal of Play* serves a role beyond its walls as a scholarly publication "that synthesizes and puts into perspective major themes of play scholarship, new and emerging areas of play research, and more" (Strong National Museum of Play 2104). Both of these models show museums moving toward Vergeront's concept.

The number of museum schools is also growing; many operate within the margins of the museums themselves, especially children's museums. In most instances, the educational experience reflects a blend of theories and practices that unite the museum and the school; some schools have long histories, while others are just embarking on this new journey as educational institutions. Each museum school reimagines the concept to fit the goals and ideals of the institutions and the community.

Unilaterally, the experts surveyed here hope to see greater collaboration between museums and the early childhood community as a future goal. Kathy Danko-McGhee envisions museums playing "a bigger role in providing experiential learning opportunities," with museum visits "integrated into the general curriculum where it is appropriate" (K. Danko-McGhee, February 22, 2014). Ted Lind shares a similar viewpoint and advocates for adding an early childhood specialist to the museum's education department (T. Lind, February 10, 2014).

Björnberg imagines museums as "important collaborators to preschool, kindergarten, and early grade schools" (G. Björnberg, April 6, 2014). He envisions future museums as "the libraries of the 21st century" that "function as an important learning platform for young children" (G. Björnberg, April 6, 2014). With the "pedagogical professionalization of museums" and "didactically skilled staff," Björnberg sees trust developing between the early childhood community and museums, breaking down barriers that hinder collaboration in its truest form (G. Björnberg, April 6, 2014).

Building a stronger link between educators in formal and informal environments is a positive step for museums in which the idea of crossing boundaries to work collaboratively becomes reimagined as a broader educational community working for a common goal. Pamela Krakowski offers another point of view; she feels that partnerships should expand beyond the museum and school dyad. She suggests that by linking educators from the museum with early childhood educators in schools and specialists from universities, a synthesis occurs; with that increased understanding of the audience comes practical applications to exhibition design and informed educational practice (P. Krakowski, March 9, 2014).

Partnerships have long been a reality in the museum community. As we look to the future, it will be important to reimagine the goals, opportunities, and participants contributing to the collaboration. Partnerships of the future may indeed take on new meaning with the increase in social networking and the virtual world. Without doubt, there is still much to learn as we continue on the path toward creating powerful connections that benefit young learners.

Trend V: The World Is Changing: Stepping into Technology

Children live in a world surrounded by technology; they are exposed to a high-tech environment that drives social interactions, entertainment, and everyday functions. As we think about the experiences of young children and museums, we see technology making its way into early learning. There are touchscreens in children's galleries and video conferences connecting preschool classrooms with museum educators. But this connection to technology is still relatively untested for this audience, and is a topic that deserves more attention.

As global perspectives analyst Göran Björnberg looks to the future, he sees a move toward a more visual society (smartphones, tablets, computer interactives), and technology that fits with the visual nature of museum environments (B. Björnberg, April 6, 2014). This integration of technology into the practice of museums is evident and growing. What we see is that a visit to the museum is no longer a casual stroll through the gallery, looking at artifacts and reading labels. It is now a social experience: teens and young adults snap photos and upload images to social networks, sharing their experiences with others visually and in text. This immersion in technology touches everyone. The world of young children is no longer limited to play at the park or drawing chalk pictures on sidewalks, but involves technology in some way. We see toddlers in strollers absorbed by images on iPads and interacting with technology in ways that stymie some of the older generation.

Museums are clearly experimenting with technology that includes a wide variety of techniques for young learners. The National Air and Space Museum in Washington, DC, connects with preschoolers in classrooms outside of the museum through video conferencing, where three- and four-year-olds learn about space travel and astronauts in *Dressing for Space*. Puppets "Sunny the Sun" and "Astronaut Bob" explore the idea of dressing for space in a 35-minute interactive lesson.

The National Gallery of Art offers interactive art activities designed for the younger set on the NGAkids website (and on free CDs). The easy drag-and-drop techniques of *Jungle* fit the developmental level of most three-year-olds, while children with slightly more sophisticated small motor skills can easily manipulate the found objects in *Sea-Saws* to create animated scenes and characters. The long-term success of NGAkids has inspired new technology-based initiatives. The National Gallery of Art is currently producing an iPad app for children to encourage exploration and discovery in a format suitable for the under-five crowd.

The Museum of Modern Art (MoMA) in New York City encourages kids to get creative with the MoMA Art Lab iPad app, where children are guided by an alien to connect with the art in the galleries in *Destination: Modern Art*. In another MoMA app, children create their own artworks using color, line, and shape, a popular approach with this age group.

The Children's Museum of Indianapolis offers the Playscape app to extend the museum experience by offering four activities for young children to use at home. Through technology children are encouraged to create a nature collage, play with fireflies, help fish navigate obstacles in a stream, and design a contraption that guides balls down a path. Experiences from the *Playscape* exhibit thus continue long after the trip to the museum ends.

An app such as *KIDZOO*, while not specifically designed for museums, complements museum experiences and serves as an introduction to animals and their sounds before a trip to the zoo or as a reminder of experiences after the visit. There are also educational apps that highlight dinosaurs, building excitement and raising questions about dinosaurs prior to visiting exhibitions found in many natural history museums. Technology is becoming part of the museum experience for many families.

As we analyze this new digital world, educators will be making decisions about how social media and interactive learning through technology are woven into early learning programming. Experts will debate and question the place of technology in mainstream early childhood practice. But what will guide educators in making these decisions?

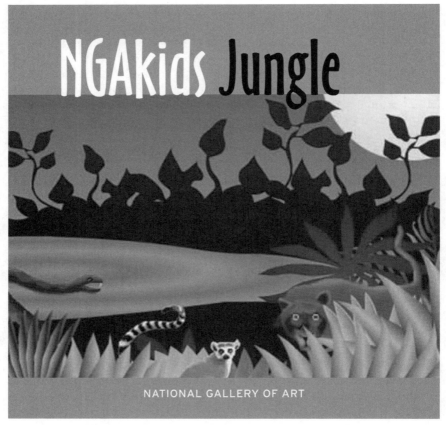

Figure 7.1. NGAkids Jungle. © Board of Trustees, National Gallery of Art, Washington, DC.

A joint position statement by the National Association for the Education of Young Children and the Fred Rogers Center for Early Learning and Children's Media at Saint Vincent College (2012) provides a starting point for the discussion. Guidelines suggest that technology can be an effective tool for learning when used in a developmentally appropriate manner. Training for educators working with children is also essential for understanding the limitations related to technology as well as special considerations for infants and toddlers. The statement concludes that exposure to technology helps develop skills just as listening to books is part of early literacy, but that digital experiences "should not replace activities such as creative play, real-life exploration, physical activity, outdoor experiences, conversation, and social interactions that are important for children's development" (NAEYC and Fred Rogers Center 2012, p. 5).

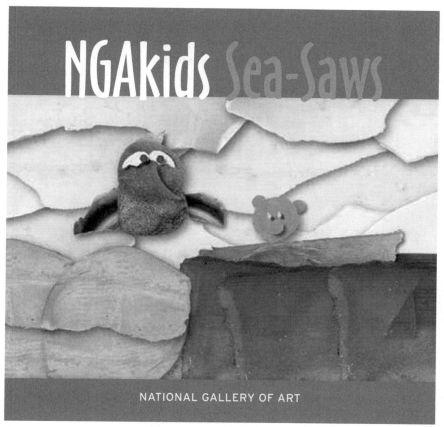

Figure 7.2. NGAkids Sea-Saws. © Board of Trustees, National Gallery of Art, Washington, DC.

The Association of Children's Museums is also engaged in conversation about the role of technology in children's museums and thinking seriously about when technology enhances learning yet continues to engage young visitors in a developmentally appropriate way. Children's museums are experimenting with technology and have successfully brought digital experiences into the lives of children in recent years with four programs honored by ACM's Promising Practice Awards. According to Laura Huerta Migus, ACM Executive Director, there is growing interest in transmedia storytelling, where multiple platforms are used to tell a narrative or story using digital technologies; it could be a technique to consider for the future. An important part of transmedia storytelling is the real-world experience, something that museums offer through exhibition spaces.

Because it is such a fast-moving trend, the expansion of technology will precede our comfort and knowledge about its place in education. There will likely be ardent debates over technology in early learning and how it fits with developmentally appropriate practice. As a field, we will be redefining our ideas from the past to mesh with the technological advances that society embraces. What seems to be clear, even to those uncertain of the role of technology in early learning, is that a technology-driven world is an integral element of today's society and a topic that will require considerable thought.

Hope for the Future: Different Expectations for Different Places

The hopes and dreams for early learning are not the same across all communities, but rather are defined by the context of culture and place. Rural areas with limited resources may have different expectations for their museum–school partnerships than larger, urban areas. Advances in technology such as three-dimensional printing may serve as an equalizing force that enhances partnerships and opens new avenues for collaboration. Although there are unequal circumstances that alter possibilities for museum–school partnerships, the future holds new possibilities. It is with hope and a belief that learning can be enriched through new initiatives that we approach the years ahead.

With the ideal of universal support and investment in early learning as a future goal, the methods institutions use to fulfill that outcome will differ across museums depending on time, funding, and space. An institution with small galleries might think about ways to serve young learners outside of the museum or develop programs that optimize available spaces, from outdoor gardens to atriums, but still show support for this audience.

Expectations also differ across geographic and cultural regions. At ACC, Susan Day concentrates on new opportunities to serve young children in the community. She notes that while the museum houses an important, world-class collection and opens its doors to the Kuwaiti community, "museums are not part of the traditional culture of the region," even though "Kuwaitis are very well educated and travel abroad often," frequently visiting museums during travel (S. Day, April 30, 2014). At home, Kuwaitis tend to rely on school visits to ensure that their children have that experience. Defining success for Day requires a shift in cultural perspective and a change in behavior related to museum visits by the public. To build a meaningful relationship with families in the community, Day shapes education at ACC by introducing toddlers to the collections through story time and providing weekly sessions of Children's Art Workshop for preschoolers, kindergartners, and children up to the age of 12. She hopes that as children and families participate in these activities, they develop a bond with the museum and see the institution as part of their social and intellectual experience.

Museums have the capacity to play a vital role in society, enriching the lives of community members and inspiring people to learn. At times, benefits are the consequence of collaboration with external entities. Some partnerships are funded by generous organizations in the community and ultimately touch the lives of many people. One such organization is PNC, a civic-minded banking corporation willing to make a difference in the lives of children, an investment they are confident will reap dividends in the future. In 2004, the PNC Foundation set the bar high with a corporate-wide investment in early childhood education, creating a $350 million initiative to support America's children. Many of the partnerships funded through the PNC Foundation Grow Up Great initiative bring together museums and early childhood programs to prepare children for the future. The PNC Foundation generously supports children's museums and has innovative partnerships with science museums such as the Franklin Institute in Philadelphia and the Smithsonian Institution's National Air and Space Museum, and collaborations with art institutions like the Barnes Foundation and the Cleveland Museum of Art. As an advocate for our youngest citizens, the PNC Foundation invests in children, with particular emphasis on those from lower socioeconomic neighborhoods.

As we envision the future, it is important to hear from the community, learn from their experiences, and understand their interests, ideals, and values. Successes should be celebrated and included in our future vision.

Making a Difference

Stories abound that illustrate the powerful impact that museum experiences have on the lives of young children. Donna Tobey at Palm Beach Day Academy celebrates the museum–school partnerships at PBDA and is thrilled with the success of the past three years. According to Tobey, these new collaborative efforts with multiple cultural institutions "reveal that there is strong potential for supporting and enriching existing curriculum," and "opportunities to create powerful, *new* learning experiences that cannot always be replicated in the classroom setting in a school" (D. Tobey, May 13, 2014). What excites educators at PBDA is the opportunity to "expand the walls of the classroom and enrich a child's educational experience" through thoughtful museum excursions (D. Tobey, May 13, 2014).

Tobey illustrates the power of museums in the life of a young child who has been inspired by a museum partnership:

Though only a kindergartner, one young boy, reticent by nature, asked his parents to go to the art museum one Saturday morning. Once there, he proceeded to take them on a tour, explaining various works of art along the way. His parents could feel the connection he felt to the art museum. He was able to truly demonstrate his understanding of certain pieces of art and the workings of the museum in general. This was a shining moment of confidence in his life.

The lives of many children are forever changed through powerful experiences in museums. If not for the exposure through school programs, many children would miss the opportunity entirely. This is true for one four-year-old enrolled in an urban Head Start program. He entered an art gallery for the first time during a multivisit program at the Corcoran Gallery of Art in Washington, DC, and discovered a new and exciting world. Though he was typically disengaged in the classroom, this young boy proudly announced that one day he wanted to be the person to hang the paintings on the walls and tell people about them. His expressive vocabulary grew with each visit and his enthusiasm for learning became noticeable in his interactions at school. This moment in time exemplifies an incredible shift in thinking; the experience became a possibly life-altering source of inspiration and excitement for a young child visiting an art museum for the first time.

These anecdotes are not unlike other stories from across the nation and around the world—young boys and girls visiting museums representing every discipline—in which children's lives are changing and their futures made brighter because of experiences in museums. For all of us, it is a time to celebrate the good work happening in early learning and reach even higher to touch the lives of more children in meaningful ways.

Conclusion

The ideas in this book are not new. As we contemplate current practice in museums and envision the future, our past is always with us. Ideas from the past resurface to influence our thinking and are rekindled with a new vantage point reflecting today's perspective. Our work as a field is to look forward while analyzing valuable contributions from the past to understand and thereby inform our vision for the days ahead.

We have come a long way since Secretary Langley opened the doors to The Children's Room on the National Mall, foreshadowing future expectations for children in museums and inspiring others in the field to explore opportunities for younger visitors.

Today, museums across the nation and around the world are engaging young children in their galleries and classrooms; some have a lengthy history in this effort, and others are new to the challenge. We learn from one another and hopefully move forward with an open mind about what lies ahead. The future story is not yet written, but it seems clear to those committed to early learning that opportunities are endless when museums welcome young children and respect their capacity to learn. Today we celebrate and appreciate the museum as a place that delights, inspires, and intrigues. We also look to the future with great anticipation for what is to come.

Module I: Museum Goals: A Conversation

Is the museum experience about learning, or rather about a fun-filled after-noon with family members? Is the visit intended to broaden horizons, or to allow a child to explore a personal interest? What do we want for children visiting a museum? As educators, it is important that we are thoughtful in defining goals that benefit young museumgoers. We begin by pondering this seemingly simple question: In an ideal world, what outcomes do we want for our young visitors? We can extend our thinking by asking: In an ideal world, what outcomes do we want for our young visitors and their adult partners?

Discuss the question(s) with your small group and list your ideas to share.

_____

_____

_____

_____

_____

_____

_____

Module II: Understanding Audience

Characteristics of Young Children

Young children see the world in a way that is qualitatively different from adults. For anyone who has spent time with very young children, it is apparent that they possess a natural curiosity and a desire to learn. They have a zest for exploring their world and make meaning through their encounters with the environment. Through our own observations, we can describe characteristics of young children and consider how this contributes to learning.

Describe characteristics or attributes of children:

_____

_____

_____

_____

_____

_____

_____

Family Learning

Although family audiences have been part of museums for some time, research in the 1980s "identified families as a major audience and unique learning group of mixed ages and backgrounds" (Falk and Dierking 2013, p. 150). Extend your conversation beyond the young child and begin to think about family groups. Discuss the following questions at tables.

1. How do families spend their time in museums? What behaviors are typical? _____

   _____

   _____

   _____

2. How do adults in family groups typically define the purpose of the museum experience? How is a child's purpose the same or different? How do individual goals influence behavior?

   _____

   _____

   _____

3. Research suggests "families attempt to find shared meaning in exhibitions" (Falk and Dierking 2013, p. 151). What strategies might facilitators introduce to engage families in finding *shared meaning*?

   _____

   _____

   _____

Module III: Educational Theories and Theorists

Current thinking in museums reflects a constructivist approach to learning, which suggests that knowledge is constructed within the individual and is unique to each person. Identify critical beliefs about learning for each theorist (provide quotes from each theorist to analyze).

John Dewey (1859–1952)　　　_____

Lev Vygotsky (1896–1934)　　　_____

Maria Montessori (1870–1952)　_____

Jean Piaget (1896–1980)　　　　_____

Jerome Bruner (1915—)　　　　_____

Howard Gardner (1943—)　　　_____

Describe constructivist learning in your own words. Share with your small group.

_____

_____

Quotes from Selected Educational Theorists

- We do not learn from experience . . . we learn from reflecting on experience.—Dewey
- Education is a social process; education is growth; education is not preparation for life but is life itself.—Dewey
- What children can do with the assistance of others might be in some sense even more indicative of their mental development than what they can do alone.—Vygotsky
- A child's greatest achievements are possible in play, achievements that tomorrow will become her basic level of real action and morality.—Vygotsky
- Children have real understanding only of that which they invent themselves, and each time that we try to teach them something too quickly, we keep them from reinventing it themselves.—Piaget

Engaging Young Children in Museums, by Sharon E. Shaffer, 158–159. © 2015 Left Coast Press, Inc. All rights reserved.

- During the earliest stages the child perceives things like a solipsist who is unaware of himself as a subject and is familiar only with his own actions.—Piaget
- The idea of multiple intelligences comes out of psychology. It's a theory that was developed to document the fact that human beings have very different kinds of intellectual strengths and that these strengths are very, very important in how kids learn and how people represent things in their minds, and then how people use them in order to show what it is that they've understood.—Gardner

Overview of Key Concepts from Selected Theorists

John Dewey	Experiential learning through interaction with the environment; hands-on; learning by doing; new knowledge builds on prior knowledge; authentic learning
Lev Vygotsky	Socially mediated learning; constructed meaning through language and culture; grouping words and ideas based on similarities; abstract thinking as outcome of play
Jean Piaget	Sensory-based learning; symbolic representation in play; literal interpretation of the world; egocentric beings
Maria Montessori	Real-world connections; sensory exploration; respect for the child; beauty in a child's world; child-centered materials
Jerome Bruner	Internal construction of knowledge through experience; discovery learning; multiple modes of remembering
Howard Gardner	Different strengths and entry points for knowing and expressing ideas; multiple intelligences

The Early Learning Model

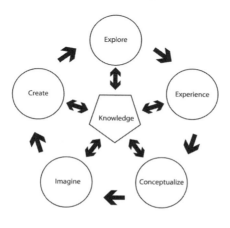

Module IV: Object-Based Learning: Every Object Tells a Story

Museum educators are well known for saying that every object tells a story. But what is the significance of the object, and in what way do objects contribute to meaning making? We can begin to understand the power of the object as we examine the hidden meanings and multiple attributes that are present in objects.

What Do We Know about Objects?

- Objects tell stories
- Objects connect us to people, places, and events
- Objects elicit emotions connected to experience
- Objects have purpose or function
- Objects are symbolic or serve as metaphors
- Objects offer insight or a new way of seeing
- Objects are concrete representations and can serve as an entry point for understanding abstract ideas
- Objects have value: sentimental, monetary, cultural, historic, and personal

Museum Experience

Select an object in the museum that has appeal and interest for your group. Make note of different characteristics that can be attributed to the artifact. What discoveries did you make that were surprising to you? _____

_____

_____

_____

_____

Module V: Interpretation in the Museum: Teaching Strategies

What experiences do you have with early learning? What does each strategy mean to you? What does this look like in museums? Share your ideas in small groups.

Thematic experiences _____
_____
_____

Learning to look _____
_____
_____

Inquiry _____
_____
_____

Play_____
_____
_____

Sensory exploration _____
_____
_____

Storytelling _____
_____
_____

Thematic Experiences

Young children make sense of their world through associations. They look for similarities and differences to identify how objects and experiences are related. Identify a theme within your museum that might be interesting to young children. Incorporate three to five objects from various exhibits into your program, all connected by the common theme.

Exploring Themes in Exhibitions

Object   **Exhibition**

_____   _____

_____   _____

_____   _____

_____   _____

_____   _____

Family Gallery Activity

Select one artifact and develop an idea for an independent family experience in the gallery. Make a list of simple objects, games, puzzles, or stories that fit the theme of the artifact.

_____

_____

_____

_____

Learning to Look

Look carefully at each object and then compare. Document your findings in this Venn diagram. Attributes that are the same for both objects are written in the intersecting area. Attributes that are specific to one of the objects are written only in the circle representing that object.

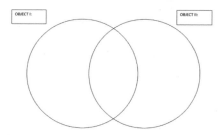

Identify two objects in the museum and compare. Document your findings.

Play

Identifying potential scenarios for play requires adults to suspend reality and think beyond the artificial parameters that so neatly define how they see the world. Take a walk through the galleries and think about possible character roles for dramatic interpretation or in the case of the art museum look to the artist as the inspiration. What other opportunities exist to bring play into interpretation? What props would you need, if any? Be creative and keep an open mind.

Exhibit/Idea for Play   Props/Prompts

_____ _____
_____ _____
_____ _____
_____ _____
_____ _____
_____ _____
_____ _____

Sensory Exploration

For exhibitions that focus primarily on the visual experience, educators can add other sensory-rich elements that will engage children more fully. A sense of touch adds a meaningful dimension to almost any gallery experience and can easily be implemented with a collection of teaching objects that visitors can explore. Sounds and smell further enhance the learning. Look for opportunities to create multisensory experiences for young children and their families, whether in programming or independent experiences.

Exhibit/Objects   Sensory Experience Enhancement

_____ _____

_____ _____

_____ _____

_____ _____

_____ _____

                                                _____

Storytelling

Storytelling is an accepted method of teaching and aligns with ways that children naturally connect with their world. It is a technique that makes sense for museum programming for young learners. Identify themes represented by exhibitions in your museum and select one for storytelling. What children's books might support ideas represented in the exhibition? Are the books age-appropriate and engaging? Ask each participant to bring three to five favorite children's books for this session. Visit the library to have an assortment of children's books available.

Museum Themes   Children's Book Title/Author

_____   _____

_____   _____

_____   _____

_____   _____

_____   _____

_____   _____

Small group discussion: Two individuals read the same story to a group of children. One reading is wildly successful, while the other falls flat. What makes the difference?

References

Adams, M. 2011. "Family Learning in Interactive Galleries Research Project Three: Museum Case Study Summary." Unpublished report for the Family Learning in Interactive Galleries Project (FLING). Annapolis, MD: Audience Focus, Inc.

Adams, M., and T. Moussouri. 2002. "The Interactive Experience: Linking Research and Practice." Paper presented at the Interactive Learning in Museums of Art and Design Conference, London, May 17–18.

Alexander, E. P. 1996. *Museums in Motion: An Introduction to the History and Functions of Museums.* Walnut Creek, CA: AltaMira Press.

American Association of Museums. 1992. *Excellence and Equity: Education and the Public Dimension of Museums.* Washington, DC: American Association of Museums.

Association of Children's Museums (ACM). 2012. "Reimagining Children's Museums Leadership Pre-Conference Proceedings (Report)." Arlington, VA: Association of Children's Museums.

———. 2013. The Learning Value of Children's Museums Research Agenda Symposium. September 10–11, Arlington, VA. Retrieved from *http://www.childrensmuseums. org/images/PlayingforKeeps/symposium%20agenda.pdf* (accessed September 6, 2014).

———. 2014a. "About ACM." Retrieved from *http://www.childrensmuseums.org/about -acm.html* (accessed September 17, 2014).

———. 2014b. "Why Visit a Children's Museum?" Retrieved from *http://www.child-rensmuseums.org/childrens-museum-facts/why-visit-a-childrens-museum.html* (accessed September 6, 2014).

Audet, R. H. 2005. "Inquiry: A Continuum of Ideas, Issues, and Practices." In *Integrating Inquiry Across the Curriculum,* edited by R. H. Audet and Linda K. Jordan, pp. 5–16. Thousand Oaks, CA: Corwin Press.

Bell, Philip, Bruce Lewenstein, Andrew W. Shouse, and Michael A. Feder, eds. 2009. *Learning Science in Informal Environments: People, Places, and Pursuits.* Committee on Learning Science in Informal Environments, National Research Council. Washington, DC: National Academies Press.

Blackmon, C. P. 1987. "The Evolution of the Place for Wonder: What's the Next Step?" *The Journal of Museum Education* 12(2):6–8.

Brosterman, N. 1997. *Inventing Kindergarten.* New York: Henry N. Abrams, Inc.

Bruner, J. S. 1960. *The process of Education: A Landmark in Educational Theory.* Cambridge, MA: Harvard University Press.

———. 1966. *Toward a Theory of Instruction.* Cambridge, MA: Belkapp Press.

———. 1996. *The Culture of Education.* Cambridge, MA: Harvard University Press.

Carpenter, Stephen. 1998. *The Three Billy Goats Gruff.* New York: HarperCollins.

Carr, D. 1999. "The Need for the Museum." *Museum News* 78(2):31–35, 56–57.

Carson, R. L. 1956. *The Sense of Wonder.* New York: HarperCollins Publishers.

Chalufour, I., and K. Worth. 2004. *Building Structures with Young Children* [The Young Scientist series]. St. Paul, MN: Redleaf Press.

Children's Museum Pittsburgh. 2014. "MAKESHOP." Retrieved from *https://pitts burghkids.org/exhibits/makeshop* (accessed September 4, 2014).

Clarke, J. H. 2002. *Looking at Art Together: Families and Lifelong Learning.* Chicago, IL: The Art Institute of Chicago.

Clough, Wayne G. 2011. *Increasing Scientific Literacy: A Shared Responsibility.* Washington, DC: Smithsonian Institution. Retrieved from *http://www.si.edu/About/Increasing -Scientific-Literacy* (accessed September 6, 2014).

Cooney, W., C. Cross, and B. Trunk. 1993. *From Plato to Piaget: The Greatest Educational Theorists from Across the Centuries and Around the World.* Lanham, MD: University Press of America.

Copple, C., ed. 2001. *NAEYC at 75: Reflections on the Past . . . Challenges for the Future.* Washington, DC: National Association for the Education of Young Children.

Crews, D. 2011. *Freight Train.* New York: HarperCollins.

Crowley, K., and J. Galco. 2001. "Family Conversations and the Emergence of Scientific Literacy." In *Designing for Science: Implications for Everyday, Classroom, and Professional Settings,* edited by K.Crowley, C. Schunn, and T. Okada, pp. 393–413. Mahwah, NJ: Lawrence Erlbaum.

Csikszentmihalyi, M., and K. Hermanson. 1999. "Intrinsic Motivation in Museums: Why Does One Want To Learn?" In *The Educational Role of the Museum* (second edition), edited by E. Hooper-Greenhill, pp. 146–160. London: Routledge.

Czajkowski, J. W., and S. H. Hill. 2008. "Transformation and Interpretation: What Is the Museum Educator's Role?" *The Journal of Museum Education* 33(3):255–263.

Dallas Museum of Art (DMA). 2013. "Museum History." Retrieved from *http://www .dallasmuseumofart.org/about/museum-history* (accessed September 4, 2014).

Danko-McGhee, Kathy. 2013. "Babes in Arms." *Museum* (Sept.–Oct.). Retrieved from *http://onlinedigeditions.com/article/Babes+In+Arms/1481143/0/article.html* (accessed September 21, 2014).

DeCordova Museum and Sculpture Gardens. 2014. "Lincoln Nursery School." Retrieved from http://www.decordova.org/lincoln-nursery-school.

Denver Art Museum. 2002. "Families and Art Museums." Retrieved from http://www .denverartmuseum.org/sites/all/themes/dam/files/family_programs1.pdf (accessed September 1, 2014).

———. 2013. "Kids & Their Grownups: New Insights on Developing Dynamic Museum Experiences for the Whole Family." Retrieved from *http://www.denverartmuseum .org/sites/all/themes/dam/files/family programs1.pdf.*

———. 2014. "Mission & History." Retrieved from *http://denverartmuseum.org/about /mission-history* (accessed May 30, 2014).

Dewey, J. 1897. "My Pedagogic Creed." *School Journal* 54(3):77–80.

———. 1900. *The School and Society.* Chicago, IL: The University of Chicago Press.

———. 1916. *Democracy and Education.* New York: MacMillan Company.

Din, H. W. 1998. "A History of Children's Museums in the United States, 1899–1997: Implications for Art Education and Museum Education in Art Museums." Unpublished doctoral dissertation. Columbus, OH: Ohio State University.

Dixon-Krauss, L. 1996. *Vygotsky in the Classroom: Mediated Literacy Instruction and Assessment.* White Plains, NY: Longman Publishers.

Douglas, C. J. 1921. "A Museum for Children." *Museum Work* 3–4:158–162.

Durbin, G., S. Morris, and S. Wilkinson. 1990. *Learning from Objects.* London: English Heritage.

Dworkin, M. S. 1959. *Dewey on Education: Selections.* New York: Teachers College Press.

Eberle, S. G. 2008. "How a Museum Discovered the Transforming Power of Play." *The Journal of Museum Education* 33(3):263–272.

ECAE (Early Childhood Art Educators). 2000. "Art: Essential for Early Learning." Early Childhood Art Educators (ECAE) Issues Group, National Art Education Association Position Paper. Retrieved from *http://www.arteducators.org/community /committees-issues-groups/ECAE_Position_Statement.pdf* (accessed September 6, 2014).

Edwards, C., L. Gandini, and G. Forman, eds. 2012. *The Hundred Languages of Children: The Reggio Emilia Experience in Transformation.* Santa Barbara, CA: Praeger, ABC-CLIO.

Eisner, E. 1985. "Aesthetic Modes of Knowing." In *Learning and Teaching: The Ways of Knowing*, edited by E. Eisner, pp. 23–36. Chicago, IL: University of Chicago Press.

Falk, J., and L. Dierking. 2000. *Learning from Museums: Visitor Experiences and the Making of Meaning*. Walnut Creek, CA: AltaMira Press.

———. 2013. *The Museum Experience Revisited*. Walnut Creek, CA: Left Coast Press.

Fenichel, M., and H. A. Schweingruber. 2010. *Surrounded by Science: Learning Science in Informal Environments*. Washington, DC: The National Academies Press.

Findlay, J. A., and L. Perricone. 2009. *WPA Museum Extension Project 1935–1943: Government Created Visual Aids for Children from the Collections of the Bienes Museum of the Modern Book*. Fort Lauderdale, FL: Broward County Libraries Division.

Fort Worth Museum of Science and History. 2014. "About Us." Retrieved from http://www.fwmuseum.org/about-us-history.

Freedman, R. 1994. *Kids at Work: Lewis Hine and the Crusade against Child Labor*. New York: Clarion Books.

Gallup, A. B. 1908. "The Children's Museum as an Educator." *Popular Science Monthly* (April) pp. 371–379.

Gardner, H. 1983. *Frames of Mind: Multiple Intelligences*. New York: Basic Books.

———. 1991. *The Unschooled Mind: How Children Think and How Schools Should Teach*. New York: HarperCollins Publishers, Inc.

Gilman, B. I. 1918. *Museum Ideals of Purpose and Method*. Cambridge, MA: Harvard University Press.

Graham, J. 2008. *Close Encounters with Culture*. Bristol, UK: Renaissance South West.

———. 2009. *Which Way Shall We Go? OK I'll Follow You*. Bristol, UK: Renaissance South West.

Hein, G.E. 1998. *Learning in the Museum*. New York: Routledge.

———. 2006. "Progressive Education and Museum Education: Anna Billings Gallup and Louise Connolly." *The Journal of Museum Education* 31(3):161–173.

Hein, G. E., and M. Alexander. 1998. *Museums: Places of Learning*. Washington, DC: American Association of Museums.

Helm, J. H., and L. Katz. 2001. *Young Investigators: The Project Approach in the Early Years*. New York: Teachers College Press, Columbia University.

Hirzy, Ellen C., ed. 1996. *True Needs, True Partners: Museums and Schools Transforming Education*. Washington, DC: Institute of Museum Services.

Hyson, M. 2008. *Enthusiastic and Engaged Learners: Approaches to Learning in the Early Childhood Classroom*. New York: Teachers College Press, Columbia University.

IMLS. 2013. *Growing Young Minds*. Washington, DC: Institute of Museums and Library Services.

Jenkins, S., and R. Page. 2003. *What Do You Do With a Tail Like This?* Boston, MA: HMH Books for Young Readers.

Johnson, A., K. A. Huber, N. Cutler, M. Bingmann, and T. Grove. 2009. *The Museum Educator's Manual*. Lanham, MD: AltaMira Press.

Krakowski, P. 2012. "Museum Superheroes." *The Journal of Museum Education* 37(1):49–58.

Madden, J. C., and H. Paisley-Jones. 1987. "First-Hand Experience." *The Journal of Museum Education* 12(2):2.

Maher, Mary, ed. 2004. *The 21st Century Learner: The Continuum Begins with Early Learning*. Washington, DC: Association of Children's Museums.

Marlowe, B. A., and M. L. Page. 2005. *Creating and Sustaining the Constructivist Classroom*. Thousand Oaks, CA: Corwin Press.

Marsh, C. 1987. The Discovery Room: How It All Began." *The Journal of Museum Education* 12(2):3–5.

Mayer, M. M. 2007. "Scintillating Conversations in Art Museums." In *From Periphery to Center: Art Museum Education in the 21st Century*, edited by Pat Villeneuve, pp. 188–193. Reston, VA: National Art Education Association.

Munley, M. E. 2012. *Early Learning in Museums: A Review of Literature* (Report). Chicago, IL: MEM & Associates.

Murdock, G. R. 1987. "The Touch and See Room: James Ford Bell Museum of Natural History." *The Journal of Museum Education* 12(2):14.

National Association for the Education of Young Children (NAEYC) and the Fred Rogers Center for Early Learning and Children's Media at Saint Vincent College. 2012. "Technology and Interactive Media as Tools in Early Childhood Programs Serving Children from Birth through Age 8." Retrieved from http://www.naeyc.org/files/naeyc/file/positions/PS_technology_WEB2.pdf (accessed September 1, 2014).

National Docent Symposium Council. 2001. *The Docent Handbook*. Indianapolis, IN: Saint Clair Press.

National Museum of African American History and Culture (NMAAHC). 2014. "About Us." Retrieved from *http://nmaahc.si.edu/about* (accessed September 1, 2014).

NeCastro, Linda. (1988). "Grace Lincoln Temple and the Smithsonian's Children Room of 1901." Washington, DC: Smithsonian Institution. Smithsonian Archives, unpublished paper.

New York Times (The). 1918. "Children getting a glimpse of art." October 13. Retrieved from http://query.nytimes.com/mem/archive-free/pdf?res=9D01E0D9163AE532A25750C1A9669D946996D6CF (accessed September 6, 2014).

Oppenheimer, F. 1968. "Rationale for a Science Museum." *Curator: The Museum Journal* 1(3):206–209.

P21 (Partnership for 21st century Skills). n.d. "Our History." Retrieved from *http://www.p21.org/about-us/our-history* (accessed September 6, 2014).

Peniston, W. A., ed. 1999. *The New Museum: Selected Writings of John Cotton Dana*. Washington, DC: American Association of Museums.

Philadelphia Museum of Art. 2014. "Preschool Groups." Retrieved from *http://www.philamuseum.org/education/32-606-507.html?page=1* (accessed September 1, 2014).

Piaget, J. (1951) 1962. *Play, Dreams, and Imitation in Childhood*. Translated by C. Gattegno and F. M. Hodgson. New York: W. W. Norton & Company.

Pianta, R. C., K. M. LaParo, and B. K. Hamre. 2008. *Classroom Assessment Scoring System*. Baltimore, MD: Brookes Publishing Company.

Piscitelli, B., and D. Anderson. 2000. "Young Children's Learning in Museum Settings." *Visitor Studies Today* 3(3):3–10.

Pitman-Gelles, B. 1981. *Museums, Magic, & Children*. Washington, DC: Association of Science-Technology Centers.

Reddy, S. 2013. "Wise beyond their years: What babies really know." *The Wall Street Journal*, February 11. Retrieved from http://online.wsj.com/news/articles/SB10001424127887323511804578298202087733868.

Reggio Children. 2010. *The Infant Toddler Centers and Preschools of Reggio Emilia: Historical Notes and General Information*. Reggio Emilia, Italy: Municipal Infant-Toddler Centers and Preschools of Reggio Emilia.

Reich, R. 2003. "The Socratic Method: What It Is and How To Use It in the Classroom." *Speaking of Teaching, Stanford University Newsletter on Teaching* 13(1):1–4. Retrieved from *http://web.stanford.edu/dept/CTL/Newsletter/socratic_method.pdf* (accessed September 22, 2014).

Schwarzer, M. 2006. *Riches, Rivals, & Radicals: 100 Years of Museums in America*. Washington, DC: American Association of Museums.

Science Museum of Minnesota. 1996. *Museum Schools Symposium 1995: Beginning the Conversation.* St. Paul, MN: The Museum.

Scientific American. 1900. "The Children's Museum of Brooklyn Institute." May 12, p. 296.

Sharpe, E. 1987. "The Visitor as Historian: The Hands-On History Room Experience." *Journal of Museum Education* 12(2):8–11.

Sheppard, B., ed. 1993. *Building Museum & School Partnerships.* Washington, DC: American Association of Museums.

Shore, R. 1997. *Rethinking the Brain: New Insights into Early Development.* New York: Families and Work Institute.

Sidman, J. 2011. *Swirl by Swirl.* Boston, MA: HMH Books for Young Readers.

Silverstein, Lynne B., and Sean Layne. 2010. "Defining Arts Integration." Retrieved from *http://www.kennedy-center.org/education/partners/defining_arts_integration.pdf* (accessed September 10, 2014).

Smith, G. A. 2011. "To Touch or Not To Touch: That Is the Question!" *Journal of Museum Education* 36(2):137–146.

Smithsonian Early Enrichment Center. 2014. Smithsonian Early Enrichment Center press kit. Washington, DC: SEEC.

Smithsonian Institution. 1902. *Annual Report of the Board of Regents of the Smithsonian Institution for the Year Ending June 30, 1901: Appendix to the Secretary's Report.* Washington, DC: Smithsonian Institution.

Strong National Museum of Play. 2014. "Education." Retrieved from http://www.museumofplay.org/education (accessed August 31, 2014).

Tanner, L. N. 1997. *Dewey's Laboratory School: Lessons for Today.* New York: Teachers College Press, Columbia University.

Tyack, D., and L. Cuban. 1995. *Tinkering toward Utopia: A Century of Public School Reform.* Cambridge, MA: Harvard University Press.

Udry, Janice May. 1987. *Tree is Nice.* New York: HarperCollins.

Urban, W. J., and J. L. Wagoner. 2004. *American Education: A History.* New York: McGraw-Hill.

Visible Thinking. 2014. "Starting with Routines." Retrieved from *http://www.visiblethinkingpz.org/VisibleThinking_html_files/02_GettingStarted/02b_StartingWith Routines.html* (accessed September 1, 2014).

Vygotsky, L. (1962) 1986. *Thought and Language.* Boston, MA: Massachusetts Institute of Technology.

———. 1966. "Play and Its Role in the Mental Development of the Child." *Soviet Psychology* 12:6–18.

———. 1978. *Mind in Society.* Cambridge, MA: Harvard University Press.

Weisberg, S. K. 2006. *Museum Movement Techniques.* Landham, MD: AltaMira Press.

Whetzel, M. 1987. "The Object Gallery at the Florida State Museum." *The Journal of Museum Education* 12(2):15.

White House. 2014a. "Education: Knowledge and Skills for the Jobs of the Future: Early Learning." Retrieved from http://www.whitehouse.gov/issues/education/early-childhood (accessed August 29, 2014).

———. 2014b. "Education." Retrieved from http://www.whitehouse.gov/issues/education (accessed August 29, 2014).

Wing, Natasha. 2009. *An Eye for Color: The Story of Josef Albers.* New York: Henry Holt and Company.

Wolf, B., and E. Wood. 2012. "Integrating Scaffolding Experiences for the Youngest Visitors in Museums." *Journal of Museum Education* 37(1):29–37.

Wolfe, Caroline. 2012. "The Wonder of a Seed," Retrieved from http://www.opalschoolblog
.typepad.com (accessed October 28, 2014).

Zeller, T. 1989. "The Historical and Philosophical Foundations of Art Museum Education
in America." In *Museum Education: History, Theory, and Practice,* edited by N. Berry
and S. Mayer S., pp. 10–89. Reston, VA: The National Art Education Association.

Index

About the Author

Sharon E. Shaffer is a museum consultant and leading expert in the field of early learning and museum education. She is the Founding Director for the Smithsonian Early Enrichment Center [SEEC], the Smithsonian Institution's lab school, where she created a national model focused on museum-based education for children aged six and younger. Dr. Shaffer received the Smithsonian Institution's Secretary's Gold Medal for Exceptional Service, the only educator to receive this honor. Shaffer consults with schools and museums across the United States and abroad, leading workshops on educating young children using art, objects, and collections. In addition to her consulting relationships with museums and schools, Dr. Shaffer teaches at the University of Virginia, a position that she has held for the past 10 years. She contributes to the field through professional writing for national publications and serving as guest editor for the Spring 2012 issue of the *Journal of Museum Education* titled "Early Learning: A National Conversation."